AN AMERICAN JOURNEY

By Mal Mixon
with Dennis Seeds

Cover design by Stacy Vickroy/Amanda Horvath
Layout and design by Kaelyn Hrabak
Edited by Randy Wood

ISBN: 978-0-9839983-6-5

LCCN: 2012952739

What others are saying about this book:

"Mal Mixon's 'An American Journey' could have been titled 'Cliffs Notes for the Would-be Executive.' Mal is the ultimate entrepreneur, and he's a straight-talker to boot. He tells you what he did, how he did it and why he did it. Although he's an alumnus of two of the world's most elite institutions, Harvard and the United States Marine Corps, he doesn't embellish anything. His surprisingly candid and utterly guileless tale both enlightens and amuses. He's a country boy at heart, but don't let that fool you. He knows how to lead, and he plays to win."

— Lieutenant Governor (1978-82), Governor (1982-86), U.S. Senator (1989-2001) from Virginia and Captain, USMC, (Ret.) Charles Robb

-:-

"Mal Mixon's journey beginning in Spiro, a small town in eastern Oklahoma, goes through Harvard to the Marines in Vietnam to become CEO of Invacare and principal investor in numerous companies employing thousands of people. It's inspirational and a real motivational map for potential entrepreneurs. Mal shares his guidelines to success: hard work, salesmanship, integrity and the importance of skin in the game. Driven by his own principles, it's no surprise that he's improved the lives of thousands of people all across the world."

— Don Nickles, U.S. Senator (1981-2005) from Oklahoma

-:-

"A must-read for any young person who comes from modest means and dreams big, Mal Mixon's story reveals a serial entrepreneur that has never been afraid of taking a risk. In his book, Mal illustrates that success in business is about much more than just profit — it is about creating value and improving both products and processes. His '18 Life Lessons' are a virtual playbook on how to win in life and business."

— Jenn Higgins, lobbyist for Tauzin Consultants LLC, Washington, D.C.

-:-

"Mal Mixon's generous memoir brings us inside the world of a fiercely honest and vulnerable human being. In his uniquely American voice, Mal describes the amazing journey from the simple realities of small-town Oklahoma to an unexpected academic education at Harvard to the killing fields of Vietnam and back to the unwelcoming realities of hard-knocks America. Mal has the rare ability to see value where most of us do not, just as his own life became more valued at each surprising new chapter. Finally finding his stride as an active and successful business entrepreneur, Mal realizes that the passion of his maturity is blossoming into a career devoted to actively creating value where none existed before, building organizations and products answering need, providing employment, and generating new globally relevant institutions. This wonderful book is a testament to a life's devotion to the betterment of our world."

— **Joel Smirnoff, president, Cleveland Institute of Music**

-:-

"Mal's 'An America Journey' is a must-read, like de Tocqueville's 'Democracy in America.' Mal, a Marine combat officer in Vietnam in 1965-66, has the eye of a novelist, elegant prose, and a remarkable sensitivity to the aspirations and strategies of what makes Mal's America great."

— **Frederick H. Graefe, Esq., well-known lobbyist in Washington, D.C.**

Contents

Mal: In memory of my father, Aaron Malachi Mixon Jr., who guided me in the early parts of my American journey and died of pancreatic cancer in 1971.

Dennis: To my inspiration in life, my wife, Sue.

FOREWORD

"An American Journey" is a tour de force of a man's "life in full."

The many lessons I've learned from Mal Mixon are captured in this wonderful commentary. It would serve all of us to read his history and learn from someone who always sees the sun rising in good times as well as bad. Young people can be inspired by a "can-do" attitude that leads to dreams fulfilled.

Tracing his life from youth to adulthood reveals the keys to Mal's success — hard work, strong values, deep friendships, optimism and real courage.

We learn from Mal that the challenges of life build character and strength that allow us to make the world a better place.

Study this man's life and you will find yourself changed for the better and challenged to lead life to the fullest.

— Gov. John Kasich, State of Ohio

Chapter 1: An Oklahoma boy

I've often asked myself, *"How the hell did I ever get out of here?"* I'm talking about Spiro, Okla., a small town 18 miles southwest of Fort Smith, Ark. When I grew up in the 1940s and '50s, about 1,100 people lived in Spiro. Fort Smith was the closest city of any size, and it was the site of the federal court of *"Hanging"* Judge Isaac C. Parker who for 21 years in the late 1800s was the law for this frontier Indian Territory, which included Spiro, of course. Parker sentenced 160 criminals to hang, of which 79 were executed, more than any other federal judge in U.S. history. His sentences included the likes of Cherokee Indian outlaw Smoker Mankiller, who, if you will, was true to his name.

I love American history and have read all kinds of history books, but I found that as far as I can tell, nobody who was anybody came from Spiro — except a very few, the likes of former St. Louis Cardinals pitcher Ryan Franklin, University of Tulsa head football coach Bill Blankenship and the guy who wrote that song by The Hollywood Argyles, *"Alley Oop"* — Dallas Frazier. Oh, and me, Mal Mixon, a country boy who became a successful entrepreneur from this faraway railroad town just south of the Arkansas River. I apologize if I left out any others.

While there are several stories on the origin of the name Spiro, nobody seems to know which is true — but they all say the town was named after somebody of local importance. One thing for certain is that my grandfather's house, on County Road 1220 atop a rise in the terrain we called Mixon Hill, offered a picturesque view of the area: rolling hills, cattle grazing in the fields, lazy rivers and streams. Looking south I could see the fields, the cemetery and the woods I walked about a mile through to go to school. A little farther in the distance is the world's tallest hill or shortest mountain (1,999 feet) called Poteau Mountain. It is one foot short of officially being tall enough to be a mountain, but we all called it a mountain anyway.

When I was a boy, my father used to drive me to the top of that hill where the lodge there had a black-and-white TV that could get a signal from Tulsa. We'd watch the fights: Bobo Olson or Sugar Ray Robinson. We couldn't get good TV reception in those days down in Spiro. The guys sat around, smoked cigars and watched the boxing.

As for the town of Spiro, it really didn't offer much. It was just one of those many small American towns in a poor area that sprung up because the railroad decided it was a good place to refuel; the steam trains had to take on water before crossing the Arkansas River three miles ahead. The town sprouted in the late 1890s as a stop on what later became the Kansas City Southern Railway. When I was a kid, bordering both sides of the wide Main Street was a couple of blocks of rather dull buildings. Many are still there today, but most are boarded up. There was a hardware store called Dunklin Brothers. Another one was Redwine's and one called Hayes and West. There was the weekly paper, the *Spiro Graphic*. There's a barber shop and the old pool hall. And the Spiro Ice Co. building is still there, but it's closed. I remember ice used to come out the chute —

big blocks, which you'd take home and put in your icebox, in the days before electric refrigerators.

It makes me think that small-town America is disappearing, forever. When they built the federal highway through Spiro in the 1960s, that's U.S. 271, businesses soon opened along it. It shifted the center of the community from the old downtown to new properties sprawling along the highway.

Dedication ceremonies for new highways were always a big deal then because they brought dignitaries — and attention — to the area. When John Kennedy was president, my dad attended a dedication ceremony for opening another area of the federal highway. He told me President Kennedy said, *"I'm glad to be here in Oklahomer,"* in his heavy Boston accent. The powerful U.S. Senator Robert S. Kerr (D-Oklahoma) said, *"Mr. President, here we say 'Oklahoma.'"* Kennedy replied, *"That's what I said — 'Oklahomer.'"*

Small-town Spiro got a virtual, slow death sentence as the railroad declined after highway U.S. 271 was built. I wasn't there for that highway dedication. I had already moved on with my life. Not that I was pounding on the door to exit. I had had a great time hunting, fishing, horseback riding and playing sports. I had music, art and even ballet lessons. I made some lifelong friends. When, as a youth, it came to what I wanted to be, I didn't know. I gave it a lot of thought, but I didn't know. I didn't think, *"I want to be a doctor,"* or *"I want to be a lawyer."* I was always patriotic and felt I would serve my country, like my dad did, but I never considered making the military my career. My dad had served in World War II; he told me that he and my mother had been to see the movie, Sergeant York with Gary Cooper, and when they came out of the theater, people on the street said the Japanese had attacked Pearl Harbor. He quickly enlisted in the Navy. I couldn't imagine not serving. Maybe I was naïve, but that's the way I felt.

Moving away from Spiro was a new and exciting chapter for me. I had lived there 18 years, my entire life up to that point. But there is one more thing about Spiro — it was actually an important site in Indian history. An ancient people lived there from A.D. 850 to 1450 and built the Spiro Mounds. It's on the National Register of Historic Places. When I was a teen, my friends and I really didn't pay that much attention to the mounds. We really didn't appreciate them — we hardly knew they were there. But now I appreciate them because I think they are very interesting historically. Archaeologists found all sorts of artifacts there, and from them, they learned a lot about the civilization that built the mounds.

My grandmother was Claudia Lee Mixon. She had been the widow of Andrew Jackson *"Jack"* Collins, a Choctaw Indian, and she later married my grandfather in Fort Smith at age 28, after Jack died. My grandfather was then 40. I had two Collins half-uncles and a half-aunt who were part Choctaw, and then two uncles who were Mixons. For some reason, I never hit it off with the Mixon side. They seemed a little distant, I thought. One Mixon uncle was kind of a blowhard and the other never really did anything much. They weren't bad people, but for some reason — I don't really know why — I didn't bond with them. On the other hand, I was very good friends with Buddy, my first cousin and my Aunt Princess' son; Aunt Princess was my mother's sister. Buddy had had polio and had to play football with his arm strapped to one side. He lived with my grandmother 120 miles away in Idabel, Okla., a border town on the Red River, and he was always good to me.

My forebears set the pace

I think one of the biggest things I am grateful for is coming from hardy pioneer stock. We never really knew it, but all my ancestors seemed to have a special toughness. They were the ones who explored new lands, wanted to improve the community and further the cause of education. My ancestors have been traced all the way back to 1610 when John Mixon was born in England. He started my American branch when he came to Virginia in the 17th century, and my subsequent grandfathers migrated to South Carolina, North Carolina, Tennessee, Mississippi, Texas and finally Oklahoma, raising families while farming the land. That pioneer stock probably taught me leadership skills, discipline, patience, critical thinking and being effective under pressure.

My great-grandfather James Joyce Mixon was in the Confederate Army, 30th Texas Cavalry, Company G, during the Civil War and had reached the rank of corporal. He rode through eastern Oklahoma and fought the Union in what was the Battle of Pea Ridge, Ark. He saw that this was beautiful country. James Joyce, *"J.J."* as he was known, told my grandfather, *"Son, when you look where you're going to live, I think you ought to move there."* So my grandfather, Dr. Aaron Malachi Mixon, moved there in the early part of the 20th century when it was still Indian Territory.

He went to Sewanee College and the University of Texas Medical School. How the hell he got to medical school, I have no idea. I can't imagine how he paid for it. But I remember he had a big diploma on the wall that said *"University of Texas Medical School."* He was born in 1866, and he practiced medicine for more than 50 years. He died in 1951 at age 85. My parents, grandparents and great-grandparents are all buried in the Garden of Memories Cemetery in Spiro, as are my Collins uncles.

My grandfather was a rural family physician, and he must have been quite a character. I knew him pretty well, but I was only a kid of 11 when he died in 1951. You know how an artist puts his initials in the corner of the painting? Well, my grandfather liked his own name so much that when he delivered a baby for a family, he tried to talk the family into incorporating his name into the baby's name. I went back home recently, and a friend picked me up at the airport. His name was Johnnie Mixon Gentry. He was most certainly delivered by my grandfather Dr. Mixon. I sometimes read in the local newspaper about Aaron this or Malachi that; I don't know how many babies he helped name.

During World War II, when my father was away in the Navy, I used to follow my grandfather around like a puppy wherever he went. I remember his black doctor's bag since I went with him on a lot of house calls. One day a deer hunter had been accidentally shot in the chest and killed. A hunter drove to the drugstore and asked my grandfather to come look at the man. My grandfather went there, took a sheet and put it over him. I was just a little shaver then and I saw that. I never forgot that sight.

I also haven't forgotten the time I waded into my grandfather's pond and cut my toe pretty badly on a broken soda-pop bottle on the bottom. My grandfather sewed up the cut. It really hurt; I probably had to have 10 stitches in it. I've been told he used to cross the Arkansas River on horseback to a town called Pocola just to see a patient. When he wanted to entertain us, he played the saw, much like a violin, bending it at just the right angle and strumming it with a bow to make it sing: brmm, brrow.

My grandfather used to make me stand up and spell words while at a country store since I was a good speller. He'd say to the people in the store, *"Ask that boy how to spell that word."* They'd give me a word, and then I'd spell it. He had done that with my dad, too. It was sort of a family tradition. So I am a stickler about spelling and grammar today.

My grandfather owned one of the first cars in Spiro; he used to drive like a maniac and ran over a lot of pigs, chickens and that kind of livestock. On Saturday mornings, the owners of the livestock he had hit that week showed up to his house and said, *"Well, Dr. Mixon ran over three of my chickens."* My grandmother paid them for their lost chickens. That was a ritual — paying for all the livestock he killed with the car because they were pretty much free-range.

Later in his life, my grandfather became very religious — my dad said he was not so much in his early years, but he became more religious as he got older. He belonged to the Church of Christ, which is a fundamentalist church. One thing my dad told me was that my grandfather stopped swearing, but he had a dog he named Dammit. And in his later life, he'd get mad over something and say, *"Damn it!"* then explain to any chastising listeners, *"I'm just calling the dog."*

I don't know why my forebears chose our two family names, Aaron and Malachi. They're Biblical names; that's just what they chose back then. Malachi is the last book in the Old Testament. One time I made the mistake of telling a Jewish friend Malachi was the most minor prophet in the Bible. The Book of Malachi is not very long, just three or four pages. Well, my friend gave me a list of a whole bunch of Jewish prophets that didn't have a book in the Bible. I was surprised to learn that. Malachi was a wise old prophet and wrote about how God is just.

My grandmother introduced me to one of life's tasty treats. When I was a little boy, I wouldn't eat strawberries or strawberry shortcake. They didn't look good to me. My grandmother grabbed me and stuffed some down my throat. It was so good, I almost ate her arm off for more after that! She had sort of a wry sense of humor. I remember she thought she was the smartest businesswoman who ever lived because she raised chickens and counted all the sales as her profit because my grandfather paid for all the feed.

My grandfather was called Mal, my dad was Aaron, and I'm Mal, although sometimes as a kid they called me Ki-Ki (rhymes with eye-eye). My son is Ki, for Malachi. Almost no one went by their full name. Everyone had a nickname.

My Uncle Snook, speaking of nicknames, made a ritual out of cooking steaks. We had to go over on a bluff nearby to obtain raw hickory. He'd start a fire with a combination of hickory and charcoal, and once in a while, he'd *"walk the steaks."* That's what he called it; he'd put them on the fire for a while then take them off, then put them back on. Over and over. It was supposed to seal in the juices and give them a wonderful flavor. Well, they were great, as I remember.

Growing up Mixon

Out of the four children and three stepchildren my grandfather had, I was most fortunate to have his oldest son, Aaron Malachi Mixon Jr., as my father. My mother and father met in Oklahoma City. She worked there, and he went there sometimes to attend sales meetings. He was a salesman for the Wilson Meat Packing Co. They were married in September 1939 in Spiro. My Aunt Eva Jane (Snook's wife), the story goes, gave my mother a foolproof scheme how not to get pregnant, and I was born nine months later! Guess it didn't work. I arrived on May 22, 1940, in the back bedroom of my grandfather's house in Spiro, delivered, of course, by my grandfather. Not many people had a grandfather who delivered both his son and grandson. My earliest memory as a child is that I used to kill Oklahoma grasshoppers with a broom and mail them to my dad when he was in the U.S. Navy during World War II. He'd send me Hershey bars in return because we couldn't get them in Spiro. I had the notion that he really liked grasshoppers — a silly kid thought, you know. I used to take a broom out to my grandfather's yard, whack a grasshopper and put it in an envelope — I was 4 or 5 years old — and I mailed them to my father. I wrote, *"Dad, I know you want an Oklahoma grasshopper."* And he used to write to me how important they were to him.

I remember holding my baby sister right after she was born. I was 4, and she was delivered by my grandfather in the same back room where I was born. She was named Martha Janis Mixon, after my mother, Martha Ellen Mixon. My sister goes by the name Janis. She graduated from Spiro High School one year early, went to the University of Oklahoma and was in the marching band. She met a boy, Tom Sawyer (How's that for an American name?), also from Oklahoma — they're still married. Tom was interviewed and selected by Admiral Hyman Rickover for the nuclear submarine program. He was the only one in his University of Oklahoma class the year he was selected — and he didn't have the best grades. But with Rickover, you did not have to have the best grades. One boy had all A's, except for one C. Rickover spent a lot of time on that C; why had he gotten the C? The guy told Rickover he went out partying, and he hadn't studied as well as he should have. Rickover said we couldn't afford to have a guy like that in a nuclear submarine who had a weak moment, you know? So Tom got picked for the nuclear submarine appointment, and my sister went with him to Charleston, S.C., where they lived for a long time. Tom went out on these long cruises, six months underwater at a time — a terrible life. Today, Tom is an engineer in the Hot Springs, Ark., area. Janis is vice president for financial affairs, the No. 2 person at National Park Community College. She's a smart gal.

I think the first dollar I actually made was from running a lemonade stand at my Aunt Eva Jane's house in Idabel, Okla. So that was my start as an entrepreneur. I went there for about six weeks every summer. I had some great vacations there, and I learned each time a little more about my family. Most of my Mixon ancestors lived full, long lives for their times, and I think they possessed that combination of initiative, resourcefulness, confidence and sturdiness that was passed down to me. I was a pretty high-energy kid, and I liked to be busy. My parents used to drive me every Saturday to Fort Smith to get voice, piano and trumpet lessons — and generally, I'd have a baseball game in the afternoon. One day I was in the bi-state music festival, and I won *"superior"* ratings for voice, trumpet and piano. In the afternoon, I pitched a championship baseball game and I drove in the winning (and only) run of the game in the bottom of the ninth inning. Then that evening I participated in the Concert of Champions for voice. I'd have to say it was a pretty long day.

Talk about being focused. I remember I used to sit on the couch and watch a TV program like a western or something, and I'd listen to the St. Louis Cardinals games on the radio as I'd do my homework. I was doing three things at once — I was always able to multitask, even before that word came into use. While I was successful in my studies and in sports, I didn't think I was at all gifted as a kid — never. I thought I was just a country boy. As I got older and started giving some thought to college, I didn't think I could compete with the likes of the better-educated. I wasn't sure. I mean, obviously, I wasn't afraid. But I was apprehensive and wasn't sure if I could compete with prep-school and city kids. It's just natural growing up as a country boy — you wonder if you can compete.

I was lucky to have had a great mentor in my father. He didn't go to college, but he was very bright and read every book he could. He read all the time. He even read the Congressional Record! He was an expert speller, and when I was a boy, he'd give me 10 new words a day, and I had to write a sentence for each new word. Then he'd give me 10 cents a word. A dollar! That was no small change for a kid then; I thought it was a big deal. I learned a lot of words that way. My dad was my best friend and my role model. A lot of people ask me, *"Who in your life was most influential?"* I've met a lot of famous people, but I still say my father was the most influential.

I belonged to a Methodist church and went just about every Sunday to worship. I played piano and organ at services. My mother and I went, but my dad didn't go. The church had pretty lousy ministers, all hellfire and brimstone. My dad thought they were not what he wanted intellectually. One day, a Yale divinity student was sent to Spiro — and he was smart as hell, to use a pun. He visited us once, and we were sitting around the table when my dad said, *"I don't believe in the Genesis story."* The preacher said, *"Aaron — it's symbolic. Look at it as symbolic."* He understood my father and got him to visit the church. After that, my dad never missed one of the minister's sermons. They had a lot of discussions about the afterlife, some real intellectual conversations about what it could be. But we didn't get to keep the minister very long because he was promoted in the church.

When my father died, I looked him up and asked him to conduct my father's funeral. He started the service by saying, *"We are here to celebrate the death of Aaron Mixon."* This was a very strange thing to say since funerals in that day were always about death and somber remembrances. Today, it's common to celebrate a person's life in a eulogy. But this minister was ahead of his time in 1971.

When he left, another minister took the post. My dad went to the new man's first sermon and didn't go back. So one Sunday afternoon, I was working on my school work and sitting on the sofa. The minister came after church to visit my dad. He said, *"Aaron, I saw that you came to my first service, and we really miss you. You haven't been back for weeks."* My dad said, *"Preacher, one of your sermons lasts me a long time."* I thought the preacher was going to die, he was so shocked! That's the way my dad was.

My dad possessed some strong beliefs, you see. One time I had a date with a girl but didn't have a driver's license yet, so I walked to her house. She was older than me and had double booked her dates that night. By that I mean she'd made a date with me and with another guy who was older than me and who had a driver's license. He had called her after I had, and he drove a car, so she liked that and took the date with him for the same day she had accepted a date with me. When I got to her house, she explained to me that she was going to go out with the other guy. I was disappointed at first but said thank you to her and turned around and walked home. Of course, I never asked her for a date again.

Well, my dad really chewed me out because I didn't beat the hell out of the other guy. I started to argue with my dad that the girl wasn't worth the trouble, but he felt I should have defended my honor. His idea of what was honor was different from that of many today. My father said that when he was a kid and a new boy came to school, they selected one of their group to fight him, to find out what kind of a guy he was, whether he had any guts or not. That was a ritual. Those were different times than when I grew up.

My father never taught me prejudice, and I never had prejudice against anybody. And growing up in those conditions — Spiro was really segregated, and to some degree, it still is at least as pertains to housing. But it's interesting that I never really had any prejudices. I never saw it in my family. I had a lot of African-American friends and still do.

Another aspect of the culture my father grew up in was that you stood up for your word. He taught me that your word is the most important thing in your life. With a Mixon, he said, a handshake is all you need. You don't need to put it in writing.

When you agree with a man, you do it. He wanted me to know that the Mixon name meant something, that the Mixon family always told the truth. You could always count on us. Keeping your word will follow you in your life always. That's the kind of person my father was and the kind he taught me to be. I feel even today that with all my business associations that I am known as a guy who will step up, make a commitment and not back down. And I don't lie to them. There are a lot of people who renege on things or say, *"We ought to go around it,"* or say, *"I've changed my mind."* I'm pretty relentless in not giving up. If something didn't go quite right, I hang in there till it is. It's amazing what can happen sometimes when you are resolute. When you think things are pretty dim, take a step back and stay with it.

My father sometimes went to great lengths to protect our honor. The school principal punished him once as a student — he paddled him for something he didn't do. My father got very angry, went home and got his .22-caliber rifle. He came back and shot out all the windows in the principal's office. So my grandfather told my father he was wrong — he shouldn't have done that. Dr. Mixon paid all the damages — but my grandfather stressed to the principal, *"I will tell you something about my son. He won't lie to you. If he did something, he'll tell you he did it. If he says he didn't do it, he didn't do it. So maybe you learned something, too."*

That's what caused the problem. The principal punished him physically for something he didn't do. To my father, honor was a very big thing. The nearest thing that I can relate it to was that my father taught me you never, never lie. You will be known all your life as a man of honor or you'll be known as a guy you can never trust.

Life in Spiro

My parents weren't really strict with me. I wasn't a bad kid, though. I remember one time, the only time I really remember such an incident, I had the flu and felt like hell all day. My dad had taken the day off to nurse me. About 3 or 4 in the afternoon I started feeling better. My dad went down to pick up my mother from work, and so I decided to go out and fly a kite. It was cold, I was out there flying this kite, and the next thing I remember was Dad chasing me. I was running like a son of a gun, and I tripped on a root. He was so mad because he'd taken the day off to nurse me, and I was out flying a kite, and I said, *"Well, I got healed."*

I usually had to go to bed pretty early. I wanted to stay up and do things and my dad said, *"You're in the bed by 8 o'clock."* He made me get my sleep for school and was pretty strict about that.

My mother was a very good mom and a smart gal. She worked for the commanding general in Fort Chaffee for several years as a secretary when most women were full-time housewives. My mother worked, but she was a housewife, too. She got up every morning at the crack of dawn and fixed a full breakfast. My dad took her to get a ride into Fort Chaffee, which was about 20 miles away. She'd either take a bus or carpooled. I was left to practice the piano for an hour before school. My dad picked her up when she came home in the evenings. After my mom worked all day, she had to come home and then cook.

I'm sure she had an impact on me for family values and morals, as mothers do. But later when I was in business and had a family, she was never impressed with what I had done. She would ask me, *"Son, how is your family? Have you stopped to smell the roses?"* She was always interested in the family, how my family was. I think she wanted to keep me grounded somewhat.

25

My father had a much bigger impact on me than my mother did in that sense. She was used to doing everything. I remember she was a great cook and loved to satisfy her family with what she prepared. She took care of my dad when he was dying. We had a stable home life — my mother and father came home every night, my father was never on the road. He didn't accept promotions, even though he was salesman of the year several times, because he didn't want to be away from home. We lived the simple life there in that little house in Spiro.

My mother had a horrible car accident with her sister Eva Jane; it was on a Sunday some 25 years ago. They were going to Dairy Queen right by the local hospital in Idabel, Okla. A woman ran a stop sign and she was hit by an 18-wheeler and was killed. The truck in turn crashed into my mother's car head-on. The force caused her seatbelt to rip her stomach open. I was at the Invacare Corp. plant in Mexico when I got a call from a doctor who said I ought to come back because he didn't think she was going to live. She did, but I think she never really recovered from that.

My dad taught me how to shoot at about age 8, and I became a good shot. Occasionally, I bagged a squirrel, quail or rabbit. I had a BB gun, yes, a Daisy Red Ryder. I must have killed a million birds with my BB gun. I'd shoot blackbirds, sparrows and crows — no songbirds though. I graduated to a .410 shotgun, that's a little feller as far as shotguns go. My father gave me one shell, and I crawled through the fence and went out quail hunting or for anything I wanted to shoot with that one shell. Then I had to go back to the house and get another shell. He didn't let me have more — that's how he started me off. Eventually, I was able to have a larger gauge shotgun.

I later won the Grand National Quail Championship class contest in Enid, Okla. I'm very proud of that feat, and in a way, it was the foundation for my interest in buying a ranch in Texas. I shoot quail there, primarily. This was all some years ago before I had my stroke. I haven't sold the ranch, Elm Creek, and I still visit there every year. Anyway, as a boy, I often hid my BB gun in the pasture when I walked to school, picked it up later and hunted on the way home. Sometimes when I'd hop the fence on our pasture, I then jumped on my horse. I could slap my horse on the left or right side without a saddle or a bridle. I got to be good at that since I had the horse beginning in the fifth grade. My dad paid $25 then for the nag. I really took care of Scout — he came real trimmed down and became a pretty good horse. He looked like an Indian pony: brown and white spotted. On some Sundays, I used to ride in the local rodeo. We used to rope goats to practice our roping. You paid a quarter for every goat you wanted to rope, and you learned how to tie and rope. On weekends, kids rode horses instead of bicycles. I had a bicycle, but we'd get about six or eight of us and go horseback riding. We could go anywhere.

I was galloping on my horse once to hurry home after a sleepover. It was raining. I was going along, crouching down like a jockey when all of a sudden I felt my saddle cinch break. I slid underneath the horse and fell off. The horse kept running, all the way through town, then another mile to my house and finally stopped to eat grass in our pasture! My mother came out to see what was wrong. Of course she knew I had the horse, so she was scared when it came home rider-less and wondered what the hell I had done. As I was walking along this rainy road with my saddle, she drove up to get me.

Being able to ride a horse as a boy helped me a whole lot in getting a summer job. I was a cowboy — really! I used to work on the ranch for a wealthy man named Marvin Altman. I'd work 10 hours a day riding a horse. We'd punch cows. I mean we'd round up cattle or run them in the pen or to slaughter or brand them. I got paid $5 a day — 50 cents an hour.

I also used to mow the grass for a lot of people's yards. I mowed four or five a day, on a Saturday. Any odd jobs, I did them to earn spending money. Then I took my girlfriend to the movie. I think it was a dollar. I had enough money left to go out and live it up.

Other than my horse, another animal friend I had as a kid was a pet rabbit. I found it as an abandoned baby in the field as I was coming home from school. It was a small rabbit; he couldn't get away from me so I caught him. I kept him in the bathroom and fed him lettuce and carrots. I can't remember the name I gave him. He grew up and became big enough to hop in the toilet. He got in there and drowned — and that almost killed me. I was so sad. You know, I'm a hunter, but I never liked to kill animals. I like animals, but I shoot birds mainly — now that's a real challenge. Maybe I shot rabbits and squirrels when I was a kid, but I never had an interest in big game hunting or deer hunting. How could you justify that? I don't like it. With birds you have about two seconds, so it's a challenge.

While my dad taught me how to ride and how to shoot, he also used to delight in correcting every letter I wrote home from college. After all, he was valedictorian of his class at Spiro High School. He would find some grammatical error in the letter, circle it and send it back to me. As a result, I have become what I think is the world's greatest proofreader. That whole experience with my dad taught me to write a perfect letter. I can still hear the things my dad would have said to me even though he died a long time ago. For example, as an executive at my company Invacare, whenever I read a letter from a colleague with a grammatical error, I circle the error and send it back with a note that reads, *"Suggest you fire your secretary ..."* I find it's very effective. It's funny how I don't see many errors once I send that note.

One thing I wished my father could have seen was how well I have done as an entrepreneur. My dad was 61 when he died of pancreatic cancer in 1971. I was 31, and it just about killed me that time, too. He never got to see me be successful, but at least he got me through school, and I knew his heart always glowed with that accomplishment. In fact, as time went by, he became the official Harvard College area recruiter. He looked for students whom he called *"diamonds in the rough."* Harvard had selected a man without a college degree to be the official area recruiter. He got two more kids from Spiro and several from Fort Smith admitted to Harvard.

I can only tell this next story of my father's grittiness because another man told it to me. When my father was dying, I was outside his room and several men visited him, his old friends who had come by to pay respects. One of them told me after visiting with my dad, *"You've got a hell of a father,"* he said. My dad, it seems, was a teenager working at this local diner and had a tall white paper chef's hat on. He said the town bully came in, and every time my dad walked by, the bully grabbed his hat and threw it on the floor. The bully did it four or five times. My dad put his hat back on and told the bully that if he did it again he would kill him. Well, the bully did it again. I guess quicker than you can imagine, my dad took his pocket knife and cut the bully across the stomach. His guts were about to spill out. My grandfather drove him to a Fort Smith hospital, and they sewed him up. He never was a bully any more. Those were wild days.

Spiro school memories

I remember all of my teachers, and my sixth-grade teacher, Viola Peck, left a big impression on me because she was such a disciplinarian. One day during recess, we got an idea. It was cold and raining and there wasn't much to do, so we thought we all should stick our big toes in the water — all for a stupid kids' game. So we made every kid stick a toe in the water. Then they looked around and decided that everyone except Mal stuck his toe in the water. Next they said, *"Have Mal stick his toe in the water."* So I resisted, and all of a sudden, a student came full-speed ahead and knocked me face first in the puddle. I was just wet as hell, and it was cold. The teacher had to send me home to get new clothes. She never let us go out again when the ground outside was wet — any water and that was it.

Ms. Peck taught us spelling and sentence diagramming, and I remember that well. I thought she did a hell of a job, looking back on it. She was tough. In the second grade, my teacher taught us penmanship. Push and pull, drawing ovals. I had the worst grade I ever got in school. It was a C in penmanship, and I was broken-hearted. I had to write left-handed, and I smeared the ink when everybody else made circles. In those days, being left-handed was like you lacked something. My dad was left-handed, and they made him learn to use his right hand to write. So when he used to throw a baseball, he pitched left-handed and then switched the glove to the other hand and threw right-handed. I eventually got the hang of writing left-handed.

Talking about throwing something … once I was eating lunch with a gal in the cafeteria, and Cooper Redwine started throwing milk bottle caps at me. I said, *"Cut it out, Cooper."* He must have thrown 50 milk caps at me. Finally, we had a fight and fists flew. Principal Butler stopped us. I thought to myself, *"Oh shoot, I'm going to get my butt paddled."* Butler used to bust your backside. He would make you bend over, grab your ankles and wham! I'd say to myself, *"Oh, Judas Priest!"* as I got whacked for misbehaving. Those were the days when you could paddle students. But this time, he just took me to the office, and he was pretty nice to me. He said Cooper should have gotten more than I gave him, but Butler was friends with my father and I got out of that one.

The academics weren't really very stressful for me — they were pretty easy. I didn't take books home very often, and so I had a lot of free time. A lot of kids today, they have to study, they have to work, they don't have time to do the things I did. But I could get A's and B's and not have to study much — and I wasn't really trying to be valedictorian. I was fourth in my high-school class. I could have finished higher, but I didn't want to work that hard. So I'd get grades that were good enough for my parents, and it left me a lot of time for music lessons, hunting, fishing and, of course, sports.

I achieved 11 athletic letters in high school. I had four in baseball, four in basketball and three in football. But I don't think anybody earned that many letters before or after for that matter. Getting into the playoffs was something common for Spiro High School.

But one time we lost a state playoff in basketball. That turned out to be anticlimactic because the preceding victory was a stunning one. In the regionals, that particular year, we took on the city of Bing, Okla. They were 24-0. We won by one point in triple overtime. I think we were 20-4 and the underdog. Coach Gerald Blankenship told us to do one thing. They had a guy who was such a good jump shooter that he almost never missed. The coach said, *"Back off him when he's going to shoot, make him shoot a set shot."* So if he tried to jump and you weren't guarding him, he kind of felt stupid.

So we purposely backed off. He'd shoot a set shot and miss the damn thing. Then he'd get all frustrated.

If you have good hands and good eye coordination, playing a sport comes pretty easy to you. I had good hands, I could catch the ball, but I wasn't very fast. I was sort of like former Oakland Raiders wide receiver Fred Biletnikoff. Throw to me and I'd catch it, but I always got tackled. Actually, I took ballet lessons for a few years to learn to jump in football. I thought it would help me be more graceful and it did a little, but I didn't take lessons for very long.

As I said, I wasn't that fast in football, except I remember when we won a game against this class A school called Stigler. Spiro was in class B, so Stigler was a much bigger school. We were behind 7-0. Nearing the end of the game, the quarterback threw me a 50-yard pass and I remember looking up and seeing the ball. The field wasn't well-lit, it was foggy and the people couldn't see me catch the ball. I caught it, scored and ran between parked cars. The crowd didn't know whether to cheer or not. I had looked up and pulled this ball out of the fog. The score was now 7-6. Then I held the ball for the extra point kick. The kicker was also the quarterback, Jim Harris, and he was later the best man at my wedding. We tied it, 7-7. It was a big *"victory"* for a little school.

When I was in the 10th grade, we were in the state football playoffs. We had never played against an all-black team. The drum major came strutting out with the band. He was Henry Lee Adams. I'll never forget his name. Man, he could do it! Then we started the game, and I looked up. There was a middle linebacker and it was rock 'n' roll Henry Lee Adams! And he made every damn tackle. We had a hell of a game — and we *"won,"* 0-0, on penetrations (the number of times inside the 20-yard line, the *"red zone"*).

I remember one night at another football game, the opponents had a star player, and he got the kickoff. Coach Blankenship told us that all our guys were to block him and as soon as he got up, hit him again, hit him again, until the ball carrier was tackled. We all hit him legally, but it put him out of the game. He got hit so many times, all in one play. Coach was very good at things like that; the individual players and maneuvering the team to win, fair and square.

I give a lot of credit to Coach Blankenship. He is a great man. His son Bill Blankenship coaches the Golden Hurricanes football team at Tulsa. Gerald Blankenship is a man of principal, very religious, liked to win, and he taught me how to win. I enjoyed playing for him, he was a lot of fun, and he also coached me in baseball.

Thanks to him I got an offer to play professional baseball. I got a letter from a major league team to join their minor league team as a pitcher. I was a pretty good ball player and led the high school team in pitching and hitting. I wasn't really a great athlete — but I was a smart athlete. I was very good at hitting and catching the ball and had good eyesight and good execution. I wasn't a big bully, but I had a good arm, and I don't think I struck out even once my senior year. When I wasn't pitching, I played outfield. But I never picked up a baseball again after I left my last high-school playoff game. I didn't take the pro team up on its offer; I never really wanted to.

I had to write a paper for Harvard about someone who's influenced my life — I wrote about Coach Blankenship. After my father, I'd say he was my mentor.

The Mixon credo forms

This all makes me think that who you are is really a collection of your life's experiences. I like to experience different things, to try new things. I think that my curiosity about things and liking people has done a lot for developing me professionally. I really don't think there is such thing as a dumb idea. If you don't encourage ideas, some of them may be crazy but one of them may be unique. If you discourage that, you'll never really get anything. If you flog someone for making a mistake, well, everybody makes a mistake at some time. Mistakes are an opportunity to learn and grow. But if you make the same the mistake over and over and over again, you are stupid. If you are living on the edge a little bit, taking risks, you're going to make mistakes. However, if you are so scared of making mistakes you don't do anything, you probably won't do anything. These are some of my Mixon-isms.

I've always tried to be the best at whatever I did. I wasn't always the best, but I was trying, aiming for excellence. I'm trying that now, and my company Invacare is trying to be the best: to have the best products, have the best people and have the best practices. Don't be ashamed to copy somebody or adopt what is better. If it's not copyrighted, use it.

Get on with life. You'll have other challenges as you go through life.

My dad always taught me that every man puts his pants on one leg at a time. I felt for a long time that I wasn't as smart or as well-educated as the prep-school boys were. You come to a point when you begin to measure yourself and you get concerned. I thought I was pretty good at athletics, and I began to realize that I could keep up with these kids and be a competitor. I don't know how to define it except, you know, if you came from a small town like Spiro, you thought all the other kids were smarter than you. Then I realized there are two kinds of smarts — academic smarts and street smarts. A lot of these prep-school kids were not very street smart. They had never been out *"behind the barn,"* and a lot of times, they just stayed out too late or did silly things. I didn't do that. I began to realize that I was pretty well-grounded, more grounded than a lot of these kids I was competing against.

I think my Spiro background allowed me to know how the common man looks at things. I can generally sense how people are feeling. I'm a good listener. I think in sales, if you're not a good listener, you can't sell. Instead of telling the customer what he wants, you listen to him about what he needs, and then relate what you are trying to sell to what he needs. Then it works.

I never had a problem I couldn't solve or that somebody else couldn't solve for me. I think a lot of the difference between me and other guys is that I try to solve something — find solutions to problems. A lot of people don't like to face their problems. You and I are the sum of our experiences, and after 18 years of living in Spiro, I was anxious to navigate the exciting chapters of ahead of me, college, military service, marriage, family and business.

I was the first student ever admitted to Harvard from my little high school in my little town where there was a lot of hunting, fishing and horseback riding. It was a rural life. So from that idyllic background, I entered Harvard College in 1958.

On to college

You might think the first student to do that should get the red carpet rolled out for him or her, but it didn't happen. Actually, it was a rather convoluted journey. I had no ambition to go to Harvard. My desire at that time was to go to the U.S. Naval Academy. The speaker of the House of Representatives at that time — Carl Albert — was from a little town called Bugtussle, Okla., near Muskogee. He was my congressman and a Democrat. He gave me a first alternate appointment to the academy. However, the principal nominee accepted the appointment. So Albert gave me a principal appointment for the following year and told me to go to either the U.S. Naval Training Center in Bainbridge, Maryland or the University of Oklahoma for a year —and then I could go to the Naval Academy after that.

Unbeknownst to me, my father had filled out an application to Harvard. I had no idea he had done it. Harvard wrote back and said that I had to take the college entrance tests. I didn't know what they were, so I went to meet the superintendent of schools to ask him what the tests were. He didn't know what they were either. So we did some research and found out that these Ivy League schools (and others) required an entrance test. While kids in Fort Smith had already taken them in their junior year for practice, they were taking them again senior year officially to be admitted. But anyway, I just barely was able to take them on time. I didn't get really good scores, but Harvard admission officials thought given the lousy formal education that I received, I did pretty well. I think they were impressed that I was very well-rounded: I had a lot of athletic letters and I was musical.

Also in my favor, that was the year that Harvard decided to broaden its class admissions beyond the East Coast. They took students from every state and a lot of foreign countries. I think I was one of four students from Oklahoma; I don't remember the exact number. But the other three students were from Casady Preparatory School in Oklahoma City, a prep school. I think I was the only public school kid. I was so enamored by my classmates, who I felt were so much better educated than I was; I was in awe of them. But anyway, lo and behold, I had been accepted by Harvard, and I joined the Navy ROTC voluntarily. I would have had a two-year obligation and would have been a reserve sailor.

I got a partial scholarship to Harvard, but I fully intended to transfer to the Naval Academy because I felt the cost of Harvard was a burden on my parents — scholarships at Harvard were strictly based on financial need. According to Harvard's formula, my parents still had to pay a sizable amount toward my education. But of course, the Naval Academy was free. So, as I said, I was admitted to Harvard. Cambridge, here I come!

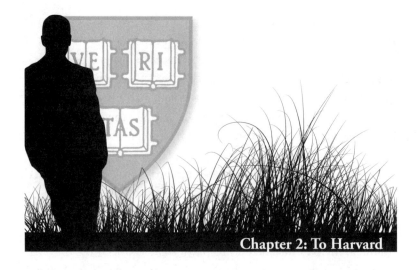

Chapter 2: To Harvard

Harvard was a challenge. I was pretty scared. Most of the other students had been to prep schools: Exeter, Andover, those old East Coast private prep schools. So there I was, a western public school kid at this premier Ivy League college — and these students were talking about subjects that were way over my head. I had never been exposed to them. I realized, too, that I hadn't studied hard enough. I really mean it when I say I did not get a good high school education. I had to begin cracking the books. I don't even think I had a date during the first six months — I had a lot of catching up to do.

Before I attended Harvard, I had never met a Catholic, a Mormon or a Jew. Then they became my roommates during my sophomore and junior years. Why had I never met them? There weren't any in Spiro. There is no Catholic church — at least there wasn't then — there was no Mormon church, there was no Jewish synagogue. But at Harvard, things were different. Clearly, I wasn't in Spiro anymore.

I lived in Hollis Hall. George Washington supposedly housed his troops in that building during the American Revolution.

That's how old Harvard is. I had a roommate named Dennis Cook, and he had already been in the Marine Corps for several years before attending Harvard. He was older than I was by two or three years. He loved to pull tricks on me because I was pretty gullible, and I just had to get used to some good-natured teasing.

Pranks on campus

So after a while, we made friends with a student from Cuba who was a doctor. He was getting a divinity degree and occasionally used to sleep in our room on a mattress on the floor. We used to drink beer and philosophize, and he became a really good friend.

One Saturday night, my buddies and I were studying pretty late, and we were hungry. My roommate said he would get some sandwiches. Unbeknownst to me, they had obtained these pills that made your urine a red color. They ground up the pill, got the sandwiches, and put it in mine. I ate my sandwich and went to sleep. The next morning, as usual, I staggered into the men's room to relieve myself, and my eyes looked down. *"Holy cow; it's blood red!"* I said.

Of course, they had set up this whole thing, but I didn't know it at that moment. I went back, and I immediately asked what was wrong. The Cuban doctor said in his very Spanish-Cuban accent, *"Mal, you know, it could be nothing, or it could be very serious."* Then he said, *"I'll tell you what. Drink a lot of water. Wait for an hour and go back and if it's the same color red, you'll have it for about two days, then it'll go away. No problem."* Next the doctor said, *"If it turns a little pink, it could be something serious."* So naturally, as he told me to, I drank a lot of water. Well, that made the urine more diluted. To make a long story short, they played me like a fiddle. I mean, I drank the water; it became pink. They had me all worried that I was going to die of something. Finally, they 'fessed up to what they did.

Another trick they played on me had the marks of a real con. I had gone to sleep one Saturday night and had planned to get up early the next morning to study. After I went to sleep, they set every clock on the floor ahead seven hours. They got me up about 6 in the morning and instead of the clock showing 6:05 a.m., it said 1:05 p.m. I thought I had slept so long I missed breakfast and had just missed lunch, too. And I said, *"Oh, man."* It was a dark, dreary day in New England. You couldn't tell if it was daytime or nighttime. I moaned to my roommate, *"Oh, Dennis. I didn't hear the alarm. I wanted to study."*

So there I was getting up early and studying like a son of a bitch until dinner time. At least I thought it was dinner time but it was really lunch time. My roommates and I went to the dining hall and suddenly I looked at the clock, and it said 12:05 or something like that. I said, *"Well, that's funny."* I said, *"The clock must be — there's something wrong with the clock."* They said, *"Oh, yeah. The clock's not working right."* All of a sudden I realized it was lunchtime. It finally dawned on me that they had pulled another trick. I must've been pretty naïve. Dennis could really fool me — he was a great practical joker.

I had to work on campus because my parents were not wealthy, and I needed some spending money. I became a newspaper carrier and started delivering the *Harvard Crimson*. I used to trudge up and down these damn tall buildings. That would just about exhaust me by the time I had to go to class. One Saturday, keep in mind I didn't know a thing about the Jewish faith, I was delivering the paper and I was collecting. I went to this Orthodox Jewish guy, he had a yarmulke on, and I handed him the paper and said, *"I've been delivering your paper all week. I'm here with your paper and to collect."* The customer said, *"Well, I don't pay on Saturdays,"* and I said, *"Well, I don't deliver on Saturdays, either."* I took the paper back and left. Then my roommate explained to me about what Saturday was for Jewish people, the Sabbath, but I didn't know before then.

Anyway, I hated that job because it tired me out, and I'd be all hot and sweaty when I got to class after delivering my route. So I left that job and took a job in University Hall, the main administrative building. I filed papers, and that was really boring. I got paid by the hour, and I hated it.

Then I got an opportunity to bartend for parties that professors held. That was the most incredible job I could ever have. I mean, I met unbelievable people — professors, heads of state and so on. There I was, wearing a little white jacket and serving all these drinks.

I met so many interesting people. There were some famous professors, even one of the candidates for president. They came from Cambridge, England, and other places. The parties were generally hosted by a Harvard professor for a guest — that sort of thing.

Home for me was one of the college's 12 houses. After freshman year, you chose your house. I was at Winthrop House, and I stayed there for three years. That is where I ended up with roommates who were Jewish, Catholic and Mormon, and I learned about their religions. One of my favorite ribbings was on Yom Kippur. I went down to a place late at night called Elsie's and got a big, juicy roast beef sandwich. Back at my room, I ate it in front of my Jewish roommates. They couldn't eat that day because they were fasting — and they were starving. I, of course, had to exclaim, *"Boy, this is really good!"*

A famous visitor or two

I remember one day President John Kennedy visited Harvard. My friends and I were still kids pretty much, and we were kind of curious to hear the president of the United States. So we huddled around the door where he was to come out. He came out, holding the door, and I remember exactly what he said: *"I'm here to check on all your grades."* Well, of course, everybody laughed. That was all he said, but I'll never forget that.

One night, I was invited to the Kennedy compound down on Cape Cod, Hyannis Port. My classmate was friends with the Kennedys. It was nothing major, but for a kid from Spiro to be present at a Kennedy party, I thought that was pretty good.

As an odd twist to this, if you remember the problems between the Kennedy administration and Castro's Cuba, you may find this hard to believe. When I was a freshman, Castro came to visit Harvard. He filled the stadium. We all thought Castro was a hero then — he had beaten the dictator Batista and freed his country. So we were very pro-Castro at that time, and then later on, he started doing crazy things like bringing live chickens to New York and all that. He was said to have hauled the chickens from Cuba and cooked them in his hotel suite.

Talking about seeing people before they were famous, I saw folksinger Joan Baez at the Mt. Auburn Coffee Shop. She performed there, but she was not well-known at the time. She became famous later on, but didn't particularly impress me then. Ted Kaczynski, the man convicted of being the Unabomber, was in my class too. He was just 16, but I never knew him or saw him.

I liked the people I met at Harvard. One of the nice things about house living was that, generally, several professors lived in the house. You could sit down at lunch or dinner and sit by somebody who had something to say and could teach you. You got to know them. You didn't just meet professors in the classroom. That was a very good learning experience.

Harvard used to have fraternities, but they were banned on campus in the 1920s so every student had to live in a house. But Sigma Alpha Epsilon kept its charter alive by going off campus and renting a property. But you could not reside there. I decided that I'd rather join SAE than a Finals Club — Harvard had something called Finals Clubs, and they were named Owl or Fox, generally an animal name. They were for men only. You probably could have your date there before a football game and then go to the game, but they never had parties with women. At SAE, it was looser. On Saturday nights, we'd bring in a band and have our dates over and we'd party. We had a lot of fun. To this day, my best Harvard friends are my fraternity brothers.

All of us went on to some great successes, and I have to give credit to the fact that our cohesiveness and camaraderie helped make us a team. We'd share our problems and accomplishments. We had rapport and genuine friendship, and knowing each other made each one of us a better person.

One of my SAE brothers, Jack Downing, went with me into the Marine Corps. He got married in his senior year in college. Jack went into the infantry, I went to the artillery, and we were both stationed in Hawaii. Jack was almost killed in an ambush in which several of his men perished.

He was one of two Harvard students in my class who majored in Chinese. He is a hell of a character. His father, a graduate of the Naval Academy, was killed in 1942 in the Battle of Savo Island next to Guadalcanal in the Pacific Ocean. There was a hellacious naval fight. His father went down in one of those ships, so Jack never knew his father.

Jack had been schooled at the prestigious Hill School in Pottstown, Pa. I remember that when he was drinking at the fraternity house, he would stand on the bar and start quoting all kinds of poetry, if you can believe that. He got his master's degree at Yale University, and went back to teach Chinese at the Naval Academy. Then he disappeared and became a spy in the CIA. Eventually, several years later, he emerged out of the network. But he lived most of his life in Moscow and Beijing. Eventually, he rose to become the top Cold War spy.

Later, when I was married, my wife, Barbara, and I went to see him in Beijing. He told me his house and car were bugged, and we shouldn't pay attention to it. So everywhere Barbara and I went for that trip in China, they put us in a separate area of the hotel because I'm sure we were bugged because of my friendship with Jack.

Along with Jack, there was Ed Rasmuson, who went on to become the chairman and CEO of the National Bank of Alaska. He flies a seaplane around with pontoons and is a hell of a guy. His grandfather was a missionary in Alaska and founded the Bank of Alaska.

David Anderson came from a family of big-time cattle ranchers in Nebraska. Once, we were in a restaurant and we decided on steak for four. I asked for it *"rare"* and he said *"well done,"* and neither of us would compromise to medium. I said, *"David, you know, you don't eat steak well done. A good steak you eat rare."* He says, *"Who the hell are you telling me how I should eat my steak? I know more about cattle than you'll ever learn the rest of your life."* But anyway, we didn't compromise. He eventually became a lawyer and teaches law at the University of Texas School of Law in Austin.

The fourth person I'll tell you about is a doctor named Tom Monath. He went to Harvard Medical School. He cured Lassa fever in Africa and was able to determine the rat that carries the virus. He has also directed research on other diseases.

The last guy is Dick Adams, who became a Marine Corps pilot and flew me through a hellacious storm to Da Nang during the Vietnam War. He was probably one of the smartest guys and got the best grades. He flew for Eastern Airlines most of his career, is now retired and lives in New Hampshire.

These five guys, with different kinds of lives who have done many interesting things, were my best buddies. We weren't above little hijinks now and then, though. One night I had been out late with a fraternity brother, who shall remain nameless. It was during the summer, after school was out, and I hadn't left for home yet. My roommate was gone, the dorm was empty and my room was packed. My fraternity brother's room was empty as well. I said, *"Well, why don't you go to my room, or I'll go to your room and stay all night?"* We decided to go to Lowell House, but we had to climb over a wrought iron arrowhead-type fence.

So wise old Mal, I admittedly was acting pretty silly, took a flying leap over this fence, and zing, I got caught on the arrowhead spike. It ripped my foot wide open. I think my fraternity brother threw up at the sight. There was a lot of blood, and the wound was large. My fraternity brother stuffed a handkerchief down into the wound and took me to see the doctor at the little hospital on campus. The doctor sewed up my foot with sutures in three layers. I had to hop around on campus for quite a while with crutches while my damn foot healed.

I'm telling this next story because my dad had told me I was part American Indian and, though I've never been able to prove it through tribal records, I am always curious about it. When I retire, I intend to research it. Harvard assigned me to be an upper-class adviser to a young man who was a full-blooded Navajo. When he was a freshman, I was living in Winthrop House and I became his mentor. He wouldn't date anybody except his girlfriend on occasion — she was also Navajo. He was a really interesting guy. His parents did not speak English; they spoke Navajo. His vision was someday to go back to his tribe and be involved in its governing process. This guy was a star football player. In the all-state football game he got knocked out of bounds and hit someone standing on the sidelines — that person died. So following the tradition of his religion, he took that as a sign that he wasn't meant to play football anymore.

We never could get him to play football at Harvard again, so the school lost a hell of a football player. Then he went on archeological digs with a Harvard professor who unfortunately died on a dig in the summer. He took that as a sign that he wasn't supposed to do that anymore. He left Harvard in his sophomore year and never came back. At any rate, it was interesting that I was an upper-class adviser to a full-blooded Native American, coming from a state once known as Indian Territory.

One thing I liked about Boston was there was so much American history around the city — and I love American history. I visited Lexington and Concord and walked the Freedom Trail. I've been to the site of the Boston Massacre and Bunker Hill — though the battle was really fought on Breed's Hill. I visited a lot of historic sites to learn about America. It's amazing to wander around those old streets — and there are so many universities and colleges there. It's unbelievable.

I want to mention the club I joined at Harvard, the Hasty Pudding Club, which is the oldest collegiate social club in America. It was an all-male organization. We put on a play every year, and the female roles were played by men. Every year, we'd pick somebody famous to receive the Hasty Pudding Award. I didn't participate in the plays. I just didn't try to get into dramatics.

Barbara and I meet

One evening, I met my future wife, Barbara Weber, at the SAE house — she had a date with a fraternity brother of mine and was a student at nearby Wellesley College. I was dating another girl. I met Barbara at a South Sea Island party. We were wearing Hawaiian leis, and during the party, Barbara reached over and pulled a lei off my neck. She says to this day that's the most aggressive thing she's ever done. Anyway, that's how we met. We started dating after that.

When I was in Winthrop House, my roommates and I had a four-bedroom suite. But in order to use the phone, we had to go in the living room. I was dating Barbara then and used to complain about having to go to the living room when she called. So one day, Barbara walked in with electrician's pliers, a screwdriver and a big cable — and she rewired the phone so that we could take it in the bedrooms. I said, *"Here's a gal who can actually do something!"* I was so impressed with her abilities.

I took her to Spiro once, thinking it might scare her off. I thought that when she saw my background it would be the test to see if she was interested in ever marrying me. After all, she was from the city, Shaker Heights, Ohio, and I was from the sticks. I took her quail and dove hunting — but it didn't shake her determination. She hung in there.

I even took Barbara a few times to *"Scully"* Square in Boston and to a bluegrass bar that used to be a striptease place. I used to go there, not to see the striptease, but they had musicians from Tennessee — it was unbelievable. They'd play *"Orange Blossom Special"* and all those fiddle and banjo tunes. They were really good. I liked that kind of music. And Barbara still hung in there.

Music was a big part of my life. I remember one of the defining times of my life — it doesn't sound very important — but I remember when rock 'n' rollers Buddy Holly, Ritchie Valens and the Big Bopper were killed in a plane crash. I recall the three of them and that little plane they were in. I was young, 18, and a freshman at Harvard. It was a shock to hear that they were killed in a plane crash. Holly and the Bopper were in their 20s and Valens was only 17. It was on Feb. 3, 1959, and I remember that because it's been called the first and greatest tragedy the rock 'n' roll world has ever had to endure. I guess because I was a musician, a performer and was close to their age, it hit me hard, and it stuck in my memory.

As much as I loved to play sports in high school, I had little time for them at Harvard. Freshman basketball was the only sport I played. I was too worried about my grades. I remember this one particular game that the coach didn't start me. He sent me in when we were losing the game. I became high scorer in about six or seven minutes. I think I made six baskets, and I tied the game. We won it by a point or something like that. So I was feeling pretty good, and because of that, the coach said, *"Mixon, you need to work more on your defense."* He didn't even compliment me. Anyway, that was about it — I didn't play in any other athletics.

Putting in the academic effort
It wasn't long before I learned that I was way behind in empirical knowledge — way behind — when I started attending Harvard. Books such as *The Iliad, The Aeneid, The Divine Comedy,* and those kinds of books — the kids at Harvard had already read a lot of those books, and there were many things I didn't know a lot about.

But I was able to close the gap. As I said, I think I learned that I could compete academically with anyone. I recognized that I had a lot to learn, so I began to try to outperform the other students, talk with them and test myself in certain circumstances. I began to realize that I was not a dummy — I learned that I was smarter on my feet than a lot of people were. Maybe I didn't have the academics, but in terms of coming to the right conclusion quickly, I was pretty good at it.

I didn't start out with really good grades. They were kind of mediocre. I was taking a course in English composition, and I was doing fair but not great. We had to write a parody. I was talking to some guys in Hollis Hall, and there was one smart guy who said, *"What have you read recently?"* I said, *"Well, I read Erskine Caldwell's 'Tobacco Road' the other day."* He said, *"Well, why don't you write a parody sounding like 'Tobacco Road?'"* The idea challenged me, so the first thing I had to understand was what a parody really was. Then I wrote a story about Little Red Riding Hood. Instead of the wolf, I made the villain an escaped convict. I called the parody *"Darling Red."* My parody started out, *"Darling Red trudged down the gully-washed road, and the heat between her legs was terrible. She pulled up the burlap sack dress to relieve the heat. ..."* I wrote it in the lingo of Caldwell. *"On her way to the house she got stopped by this convict. ..."* I don't remember the rest anymore, but you get the idea.

Well, the professor thought my parody was the greatest thing he'd ever read. I got an A on it, and he distributed it to the whole Harvard class as an example of the best parody that had ever been written at Harvard at the time. I was pretty proud of that.

One of my roommates became a doctor who now lives in Tampa. So, a few years ago, I went to my reunion, and I met him at Winthrop House. We were having lunch at our old house and he said, *"Mixon, you used to piss us off so much."* And I said, *"Well, why? What did I do?"* He said, *"You used to stay out and party, come in on Friday nights, cram and stay up all night, and you'd get better grades than we did, and we studied all week."* I said somewhat apologetically, *"Well, I didn't know it made you mad!"*

Anyway, I used to be a pretty good crammer, and I could cram a lot of information in my head in a short period of time. I wasn't as serious a student as probably I should have been. I was much more serious when I went back to Harvard Business School. I was just sort of an average B/C student at Harvard. I didn't graduate with honors or anything like that.

I thought I wanted to be an engineer. That was the "in" thing for high school graduates in 1958; if you weren't an engineer, you were nothing. Kids who were studying the arts seemed to me like they were wasting their education. So I went to a physics class, and there was this 16-year-old kid who had been admitted to Harvard two years early. This little stinker knew the answer to everything. All of a sudden, I realized that compared to this kid, I was nothing — and that engineering, math and science weren't for Mal Mixon.

So I changed my major to the easiest technical major there was — physical sciences. The credits I earned while working toward the engineering degree would still count. I was allowed to take all the arts courses I wanted and still qualify for a degree because I had already taken statistics and math courses. My grades went up tremendously once I switched.

I remember having two particular courses, one was *"Criminology"* and the other was called the *"Psychology of Intergroup Relations."* We studied South Africa and all the problems of blacks and whites that were going on there. I got this idea to write one paper for both classes. There's a town in Oklahoma called Boley, which had an all-black population. I'd never been there before, but it was publicized that they had a very low crime rate. So I had this theory that the absence of whites in this all-black town was the reason there was so little crime. I talked both professors into letting me write one paper analyzing this town from the point of view of intergroup relations and the absence of crime being the other part of the paper. I wrote to the sheriff, the mayor and teachers, and they invited me to come to Boley.

I took Barbara with me, and to condense this story, you should have seen the size of this sheriff. You weren't going to screw around in that town. This sheriff even locked up his own son once for drinking. I can tell you, this town didn't have any crime because of this sheriff. I couldn't write a paper on that so I interviewed all these people and then wrote the paper based on my theory. They told me that if there's a white man in town after dark, he was there for no good reason. He was probably there to steal or do some mischief. I wrote about how the absence of the white man was a causal factor for low crime.

Barbara told me, tongue-in-cheek, *"I thought that was an interesting experience."* Well, I got an A on the paper for both classes!

One A that I couldn't get was in French. I think I was the first student ever admitted to Harvard without having taken a foreign language, but I'm not sure of that. At least it was a rarity, because every freshman had taken a foreign language, it seemed, even Latin or something. I got a C in first-year French. It was tough. During the second year — I had to take two years — I failed the first half of the course. It was one of the few failing grades I have ever received. My teacher was the department head, a native of France, and he was difficult. First-year French was taught in French, and no English was spoken in class. I remember calling home to Spiro after the first class. I hadn't comprehended a word. Not a bon mot. I said to my dad, *"I'm in deep trouble. I'll never get through this. I just sat through a class taught in French, and I didn't understand a word they said. They're teaching the course in French and I don't understand French."* My father encouraged me to keep at it, so I plastered words around my house to learn them.

I'm sure that my pronunciation was terrible; I had a Southern accent, with an Oklahoma twang. I had to retake the first semester, second-year course. This time I was taught by a younger teacher. We got along trés bien, and we'd even drink beer together. I took a lot of time to practice my French. I got a B, and the department head, a little curious, said, *"Mixon, Mixon ... that can't be the same Mixon I had in my classes."* He asked to see my paper and wanted to grade it himself. He thought there was a mistake. Anyway, I went from an E to a B. It goes to show you that if you fail, pick yourself up and get back in the game, and you'll do well.

While I wrote home a lot, I never really got homesick. I liked Harvard. The first trip I took back to Spiro, I thought it was really going to be fun, but I went into the pool hall — I used to play a pretty good game of pool as well as dominos there — and this guy was leaning against the wall with some old fellers and he said, *"There's that Mixon kid. He's been up East to school somewhere. Princeton or Yale or Harvard — yeah, Harvard."* And he said, *"Say something smart for us, Mal."* So they had a way of bringing you down to reality. I don't think I answered, but if I had, I'm sure I could have said something *"smart"* enough.

Oh, to be in uniform

As an ROTC student, I received basic military and officer training for the Navy. I participated in regular drills during the school year and training activities during the summer such as cruises. At the end of my freshman year, the commanding officer of the naval unit called me into his office, and he showed me a film on the U.S.

Naval Academy, of which he was a graduate. He said, *"Every year we pick one student to put on a full scholarship, and we picked you. You can stay at Harvard now and we'll pay your way, but you have to commit to serving four years instead of two."* It was a full scholarship under something called the Holloway Plan. It not only paid my tuition, but it also gave me money for books. It was pretty damn nice. He said, *"You can make up your mind this summer. You don't have to leave Harvard over money anymore."* I knew what I wanted to do, but I didn't make my mind up. And meanwhile, I went on my third class cruise.

That cruise was on the USS Wasp, an old World War II aircraft carrier. We were the first aircraft carrier to go down the St. Lawrence Seaway. The carrier sailed out into the Atlantic Ocean, came around Canada, went down the seaway and docked in Quebec City. Of course, I'd never been there. But guess what? Walking down the streets of Quebec, I ran into Cooper Redwine (remember our milk cap fight?) and his brother — both from Spiro. Small world! Anyway, somewhere on this cruise, I was down cleaning the bilges of the ships. I was polishing fixtures, and in those days, the midshipmen were pretty much like slave labor. I got this command to report to the captain, so I cleaned up and went up to the captain's office quarters. I was standing there at attention, and he said, *"Congratulations, midshipman. We're going to fly you to the Naval Academy in Annapolis today. Get your gear packed."* And I said, *"Sir, I just decided to stay at Harvard."* And he looked at me like, *"Are you an idiot, like some kind of flower child?"* I don't remember exactly what he said, but I remember he said, *"Get out of my office."* He was very upset that I had turned down the Naval Academy in favor of Harvard.

The Holloway Plan scholarship included a flight training program, and if you liked it, then they wouldn't waste money on having you wash out of the program at the Naval Air Station in Pensacola. A lot of guys wash out of Pensacola because they find out they don't like to fly. And so — the Navy paid for my private license from an airport near Boston. I had one of the most exciting moments of my life when the instructor stepped out of the plane and said, *"Take it around yourself."* It was a real thrill, the first time you solo. Anyway, I had to take what they call a cross-country trip. I flew up to Concord, N.H., and Old Town, Maine, and back to Boston. That was my initiation to a cross-country trip.

I took Barbara up once. I thought I was a real hot dog pilot. There are certain things you can do with the controls — they call it a *"slip"* and you can push left rudder and right aileron, and you're flying and all of a sudden you can knife through the air like *"zoom!"* and then you could flip it back. So I was showing off to Barbara in a Piper Colt, and all of a sudden, she was looking down at the ground, and the door is on the bottom instead of on the side. She never flew with me again after that!

In the second year of my training in the military, I went to Little Creek, Va., and Kingsville, Texas. In Little Creek, we had amphibious training, landing craft on the beach. At Kingsville, we had flight training. We went up with these guys to learn if we wanted to be a pilot. They took us up and did all kinds of crazy maneuvers to scare the hell out of us. But it was no big deal.

But I learned that if I went into the flight program, it would have been a six-year stint instead of four years, and I decided four years was long enough. I wouldn't do it. Well, as it ended up, I didn't even like the ocean, and I decided I wanted to take the Marine Corps option for ROTC, which altered my last year of training. The Marines were a new kind of challenge for me. I really felt that if I could become a Marine, I would prove myself in a different way. I thought it was the best route; whether it was or it wasn't, I thought it was. I was already developing my ability to stick to my decisions — which would come in handy in future business matters.

One year — I don't remember what year it was, sophomore or junior year, after I had completed my training, I went to Washington as a congressional intern. I interned for Sen. Robert Kerr. He was a very powerful senator, a Democrat, too (My dad was a Democrat. He may have had some pull). I used to take a newsletter around from Sen. Kerr to all the offices. Occasionally a senator said, *"Sit down, boy. How do you like this place?"* I'd visit with them. Kerr took me down to the floor of the Senate where famous senators from the past — Calhoun, Clay and Webster — had sat. I got a little taste of Washington that summer after my training in the military.

That summer when I was working and living in the SAE house in Washington, I used to hitchhike back to Cleveland on occasion. I remember hitchhiking to Cleveland to see Barbara. Her father felt sorry for me so he bought me a ticket for my return.

One time Jack Downing and I decided to hitchhike — on Navy planes, because we were in the military ROTC. So we went from Boston to Westover Air Reserve Base. We hitchhiked on a flight to Washington. Somehow we ended up in Miami — and we were trying to get to Spiro. Then we hitchhiked on a plane to Dallas, and we ran into a really bad storm. People were shaking in their boots. I mean, it was lightning and the storm was tossing the plane around, it was pouring rain, and we were sitting in these hammock-type seats. People were throwing up.

Finally, we landed in Dallas, and the pilot came back and said, *"We made it, thanks to the good Lord and one of the best damn pilots in the Air Force,"* meaning himself. Anyway, Jack and I hitchhiked by car from Dallas to Spiro. We had traveled all the way from Boston to Spiro. That shows you what kids will do.

Graduation flurry

I have to say that one of the proudest moments I ever had was when I graduated from Harvard, but I was even more impressed by this: My mother pinned on my second-lieutenant bars, making me an officer in the Marine Corps. It was more important to me. I don't know why, but I'd been through such tough training. One day, I got my second lieutenant bars, and the next day, I graduated. It was June 1962. Then Barbara and I drove all the way to Cleveland and got married the following week.

One last Harvard thing I'll relate: I got invited to be on a panel years ago — I think it was my 40th reunion — and the panel was asked to answer the question, *"What do you want to do with the rest of your life?"* Here we are, 65, getting near the end of our lives. The brighter kids from the class went to work for the Peace Corps or became research people who did everything to solve the world's problems. But old Mal said at that time, *"I better get a job and provide for my family."* Now that I have money, I decided I want to solve a few world problems. So it was almost like half the class was worried about their future. If they didn't have any money, they were worried about, *"How am I going to provide for myself and the economics of living?"* Meanwhile, the other half, the ones that had gone to work like me and made some money — now they have money and it's like, *"What do I want to do with it? What can I do to solve world's problems?"* I thought it was an interesting contrast — almost a role reversal.

Anyway, I didn't have a clear idea of what I wanted to do in 1962, other than a stint in the military. I left Harvard with a four-year obligation to the Marine Corps, and I shipped out to Quantico, Va.

I went to Quantico for officer's training for six months. From there, you pick what they call an MOS, military occupation specialty, and you request the base you want to go to. It didn't mean you would get it. I asked for three things: I asked for artillery, to go to Fort Sill for artillery training — that's an army base in Oklahoma where they've got much better training than the Marine Corps and has a much bigger artillery range — and I asked to be stationed in Hawaii. Well, I got all three.

As far as my training, I finished pretty high in my class. They graded you on physical achievement such as the obstacle course and on academics. The sergeants used to run us up and down on something called the *"hill trail"* at night. The guys screamed and fell, forcing the sergeants to go out with flashlights looking for them. They don't do that run anymore, I think, but the training for officers was tough. We had several enlisted Parris Island guys who didn't make it through.

From Quantico I went on to Fort Sill, Okla., from Fort Sill to Hawaii and from Hawaii to Vietnam.

Chapter 3: A Marine in Vietnam

By the time I was into my senior military training at Harvard, I was full of anticipation. Soon I would realize my goal to serve my country. I couldn't imagine being a man and not serving in the military and not being in combat. I really felt I had to do that to prove my manhood. I'd been to a very good school and wanted to try to test myself in a different sort of way. That's why I ended up in the Marine Corps.

Barbara and I had just spent our honeymoon at Williamsburg, Va., and I had to report for duty at Quantico. It was for six months more of training. I remember the pay I earned — $222.30 a month. Subsistence allowance was $47.88 and housing allowance was $87.50. Add all that up and it was about $350 a month. It's amazing to think about where we are now and where we were then. ... Barbara and I actually tried to do a budget one time. We never could make it work, so we said the hell with it.

There was this gunnery sergeant who trained the candidates, and he would do some funny things with us. They're funnier now than they were then, though I think they built character. He would march us to breakfast every morning — in the twilight to the chow hall. We had to cross railroad tracks where the trains would literally rip through Quantico at 80 miles an hour. So one of the candidates would go on the left side of the tracks, the port side, to look in that direction for any oncoming trains and another went to the right side, the starboard, to do the same. The candidates would call back, *"All clear on the port side, sir!" "All clear on the starboard side, sir!"* Then we would all march across the tracks.

On a particular morning, one of the candidates didn't look down the tracks. He just automatically said it was all clear. Well, there was a train coming, he luckily got out of the way, and this train, woooo woo, roared by. This same sergeant walked up to him, and said, *"What was that? Are you f-----g blind?"* I'm not kidding you, he gave that guy so much grief; it just humiliated him.

Another time I had to keep a poker face was when the sergeant gave us bayonet training. It was funny and serious at the same time, so I had to watch myself. You see, this sergeant had a lisp and a stutter, and we were still young kids so you can imagine we were less than sensitive, but you sure as hell weren't going to say anything about the lisp for fear of the retribution it would bring. Well, during the training, he took a bayonet, attached it to a rifle, and said, *"Now the first thing you want to do is you want to give him the butt stroke. Foom! Like that,"* and he swung the rifle butt as if he would clobber the enemy. *"Then you want to give him the smash with the butt of your weapon and then the slash with the bayonet. You follow me?"* We were standing there watching his demonstration, foom, foom, foom. And he said, *"If you don't get him with one of those three moves, drop your weapon and get the hell out of there because you have a mean son of a bitch on your hands!"* That was his point! If you laughed, it made it worse for us all.

Our training wasn't all on the ground. The first time I ever had been in a helicopter, this sergeant was there leading the candidates. We were loaded with our packs and the whole bit. He said, *"Now this is a helicopter. Unlike an airplane, it doesn't glide when the engine quits. It assumes the characteristics of a rock. All aboard!"* Oh yeah! Ha ha! So we got in the helicopter and deployed in our position, hoping the engine didn't quit!

Even in the barracks, we were fair game for survival lessons. The sergeant played a game with us called Air Raid or Flood. You put everything in your footlocker. If he called an air raid, you had to put it underneath your bunk. And if he called a flood, you had to put everything on top of the bunk. *"Air raid! Air raid!"* You put everything under the bunk. *"Flood! Flood!"* You put everything on top of the bunk.

We came back from a field trip; I was sweatier than hell and dirty. There were about 100 guys. Then we went into the showers, and the sergeant yelled out, *"Turn on the shower! Soap down!"* We washed and got all soapy and ... *"Turn off the shower! Get in the bunks!"* the sergeant ordered. Everybody would run, and they're wet and slippery and still dirty. Then he shouted, *"Get in the shower! Turn on the water!"* We went through that several times, and eventually we got clean, but I don't think that was the point. That shows you some of the harassment we went through as young candidates. That sergeant had a knack of doing silly things like that, and he taught us well, if we took it seriously. And believe me, I did, but it really seems hilarious now.

The Marine Corps teaches you to care about your people first. Some people have trouble with that but what they really ask is, *"Do I care more about Mal Mixon or do I care more about my team?"* The Marine Corps teaches you to be more concerned about your people than yourself. That sounds kind of strange, but if you really take care of your people in the right way, they will lift you up. If your troops respect you, they will fight to the death.

For one of my first tests of that notion, I learned to stick with the team. Now it wasn't a life-or-death matter, you see, but there was a sergeant who drilled the officer candidates, and he said some really funny things over the course of six weeks. Right away, he nicknamed me the *"Harvard pussy."* That's what he called me because I went to Harvard. He thought everybody that went to Harvard was a wimp. During one morning muster in the dark on the shores of the Potomac River, there was a whole battalion of candidates assembled. As roll was being called, every once in a while, you heard this voice say, *"I hate this f----g place."* The sergeant ran down the rows to try to find him: *"Who said that?"* Nobody answered. Though I knew the guy was near me, I didn't rat on him — and no one else did. We were a team.

The Marine Corps teaches that you are not an individual, you are part of a team, and you are only as good as the team wants to be. The Marine Corps shaves your head to make you all the same. So you're not Marion Carl, *"Chesty"* Puller or even Mal Mixon anymore. You're a Marine, part of a team. They make you do things as a team. The whole idea is to sort of take you back to day one and build you up as a team.

For me to be a real part of the team, I really had to get rid of that nickname. I didn't want to be known as the Harvard pussy. So one time, we had a three-mile march with full packs and rifles. The idea was for the platoon to run and touch the mile-and-a-half marker and come back. I was a pretty good runner and had excellent endurance. I not only ran to the marker, I passed the platoon on my way back. I was the first guy back by far. The sergeant said something positive like, *"Good job, candidate."*

I said to him I would really appreciate it if he didn't call me the Harvard pussy anymore. And he never did! He never did. Since I was the first Marine back, maybe he decided I wasn't such a pussy after all. Not only that, but I think he saw that I was solid Marine officer material. I didn't even wince when he often employed a certain four-letter word as a noun, adverb, adjective, preposition and verb, all in one sentence. Those Marines who screwed up were just humiliated by him. He was really profane, but at the same time, I thought he was often funny as hell.

We had a lot of physical training, and when I came out of that, I was in pretty good shape. I found out I was a pretty tough guy. I could put up with a lot, and I was not a quitter. A lot of people, at the first sign of trouble, they turn tail. Not me.

Every Marine is given six months of ground combat training even if the Marine is going to be a pilot, in artillery or whatever. It was pretty rugged training, but I sailed through it, no problem. I was an officer then, so the instructors treated officers a little kinder than enlisted men but not much.

Shipped out to Hawaii
After training was over, I went to Hawaii. We took a ship out of San Francisco, and I joined what was called the 1st Marine Brigade and the 3rd Battalion, 12th Marines. A brigade is three infantry battalions and an artillery battalion with all the division's supporting elements; it goes into combat as a unit. I became an AO, aerial observer, whose job is to find targets for the artillery so the weapons can be aimed at the target. This is all done while you're flying in an aircraft. After each shell is fired, the AO calculates adjustments to better aim the next round.

As part of my training, I took a flight from Hawaii to Midway Island, and from there, we flew the DEW Line extension to the

Aleutian Islands. The DEW Line extension involved having a plane in the air all the way up to Alaska and back to Midway 24 hours a day, providing coverage against a surprise Soviet missile attack. The DEW Line was a string of radar stations in upper Canada, and the airplane route served as an extension of that line. At a certain point, in case we crashed, we put on what are called poopy suits; they were anti-exposure suits so you wouldn't freeze to death. The planes literally flew around the clock.

But on Midway, the real hazard was not Soviet missiles — they were the Laysan Albatross birds, which everybody called *"gooney birds."* The birds flew a little bit and then crashed. They looked like they couldn't quite get up and when they came to a halt, they would roll over. They look so gooney when they land but are graceful when flying. The planes hit a lot of gooney birds; they could dent the wings. Compounding the situation is that the entire island is a bird sanctuary. The gooney birds are all over the place and are big problems for aircraft.

One of the things we used to do was that anytime a volcano erupted in Hawaii, we hopped in the helicopter and went sightseeing at the volcano. We flew up close to waterfalls and saw the beauty of Hawaii as we were in training — not a bad fringe benefit.

Also while I was in Hawaii, we were supposed to be on 24-hour alert, ready to go into combat immediately. If you got the Romeo Recall, you had to be ready in 24 hours. Our commanding officer was a character. He was a mustang — an enlisted man who was promoted to officer, usually a battlefield commission, like what that famous soldier/actor Audie Murphy received in World War II. We were in his house one Saturday night, and we were all partying. All of a sudden, at 11 o'clock at night a Romeo Recall came down. All the officers of his unit had to put on uniforms, report to the barracks and get everything ready for inspection at 8 o'clock the next morning.

This mustang captain wandered in the office about 7:30 a.m., all disheveled. We put him in a closet and locked the door. The colonel came and inspected everything. He never opened the door where the captain was — and we scored the best of all the units. When we were young men, we recovered pretty well from partying. We eventually let the captain out, of course.

The whole world was shocked when President Kennedy was assassinated in 1963, and in Hawaii, it was no different even though we were so far away and lacked instant media coverage. I was in an AO class when we were notified by telephone of Kennedy's assassination. In those days, we couldn't get live mainland TV in Hawaii. There was a delay until they flew the videotapes to Hawaii. I was lying in bed, and I saw Jack Ruby shoot assassin Lee Harvey Oswald on tape delay TV the next morning. It was so unbelievable. I had seen Kennedy up close when he visited Harvard. Everybody knows where they were when that happened. For us then, it was like the 9/11 attacks. You know where you were and what you were doing.

In a lighter vein, I had beautiful duty in Hawaii. I got to fly, I got flight pay, and I visited all the islands. For my assignment, I was at the Marine Corps Air Station Kaneohe Bay on the island of Oahu, on the windward side. Barbara and I initially moved into a place in Kailua, and then onto the base. We were right on the golf course. I could literally hop over my fence and be on the fourth hole. Then I could play the course and end up at my house. It was right on the ocean, a beautiful course, the best beaches — I had nothing but fantastic duty. All the officers clubs on the island were amazing and several dated back to World War II. I was there about two years. And then there was a mysterious occurrence.

The picture changes

We were preparing to make a practice amphibious assault landing on Camp Pendleton in California — I mean a full landing with landing ship tanks and all that equipment like we were assaulting a Japanese-held island during WWII.

I had been promoted to embarkation officer working for the S4 (Logistics/Embark Office), and it was my job to get the ships loaded in the proper sequence. So I was responsible for combat loading, which means the most needed items for an assault were the last in and first out. Most people don't know this, but during World War I, in one of the battles which the British lost to the Turks, the ships had been all loaded wrong. That's how unaware military planners were in those days. The things they needed at the beach were at the back of the ship. There is a movie about the battle called *"Gallipoli."*

Before we sailed, I got in a round of golf. Well, I was on the green of the 17th hole, about to putt, when this corporal approached me with kind of a sheepish look on his face. He said, *"Lieutenant, we just got orders to sail the other way."* We were all packed up, the ships were loaded literally, and instead of going to California, we sailed east to Okinawa.

We were on Okinawa for 30 days. Barbara stayed in Hawaii and lived with Suzie Downing, wife of my fraternity brother, Lt. Jack Downing. We were best friends, but I didn't see him in Vietnam. He was in the infantry. Out of my Harvard class, there were Dick Adams and Downing who also went to Vietnam, and then Jim Harris, from my high school and who was the best man at my wedding. I met up with him in Vietnam.

I did a lot of flying around Okinawa to keep our skills current. I read all about Okinawa having been of high military value in World

War II. A lot of Marines were killed in the battle for Okinawa as well as the enemy. I saw what the terrain was like. We trained there, and I can only imagine what the men in World War II went through.

After the time in Okinawa, we sailed to Chu Lai, Vietnam, and were the first major combat troops, not advisory troops, to land in Vietnam. I was in Vietnam for about a year, from April 1965 to May 1966. While I was many layers removed, I served under the famous Gen. Victor Krulak, commanding general of the Fleet Marine Force, Pacific, from 1964-68. I didn't know until I read a book about it later that Chu Lai meant Krulak in Chinese. According to the official USMC history, Krulak surveyed the area in 1964 and gave it the Chinese Mandarin characters for his name. I spent most of my time in Chu Lai. Near the end, I went to Da Nang and Phu Bai, which were near the North Vietnamese border.

In the book about Krulak, the Air Force said it would take 13 months to build an airstrip at Chu Lai to supplement the overburdened airfield at Da Nang. They asked Gen. Krulak, and he ambitiously said it would be done in six weeks — and it was done on schedule! The Seabees had developed a prefab method using aluminum planks. We built it with the Seabees in the middle of the jungle and pretty soon jets were taking off and landing like on an aircraft carrier. They'd shoot them off with Jet Assisted Takeoff, called JATO.

Our artillery unit base was about a mile from the strip. I'll tell you how high-tech our operations were. When operating out of our base at Quang Ngai, we drove like hell down Highway 1, the famous highway in Vietnam, whenever we had to get there. We drove very fast because we didn't want to get ambushed. There were no lights on the airstrip. We used Bunsen burner-type pots all around the airstrip. We would outline the airstrip with them. These Air Force KC-135s flew at high altitude and dropped parachutes with flares. They lit up the area just like daylight and helped us see to adjust artillery fire. While the planes were up, we doused the pots. You could not see the airfield. I was on the station for two or three hours, adjusting artillery fire just like it was daylight. There was a sergeant sitting in a Jeep at the airstrip, and when we were ready to land, we called out, *"Light the pots!"* and the sergeant in the Jeep went around and lit them. Our aircraft landed and then we drove back to the base in the dark. You talk about driving like hell, man, especially at night. All of a sudden you're in combat, and then you're back at the camp and you're relaxing at the officers club! It was rather strange, to say the least.

My duty there was to fly as an aerial observer (AO) about every third or fourth day. I flew about 80 missions in Vietnam as an AO. My job was to adjust fire for artillery and airstrikes, once even directing fire for the USS Boston, a Navy cruiser that fired five-inch and eight-inch shells that have very flat, difficult trajectories.

I think we got hit 15 or 16 times on those flights. A lot of times, we did not find the bullet holes until we landed. I flew in Cessna L-19s, in UH1E and Sikorsky UH-34D helicopters. I flew with the Army, Air Force and Marine Corps — anybody who had a plane that wasn't shot up. A lot of times, our planes were in repair so I flew with whomever I could.

We didn't wear any combat gear, just a flight suit or camouflages. I will tell you one thing we did religiously — we all sat on a steel plate, because we didn't want to get shot in the balls. I wouldn't have minded getting shot in the head because it likely would be all over in a flash. But, this is the honest to God truth — the men did not want to have their testicles shot off. More than once that damn plate protected us. Well, you're up there, and they're shooting at you from below. You hear it.

Ping! And you know the plate saved you. It never happened to me. But other guys had close calls. I'm convinced the steel plate saved them. Sitting there really wasn't uncomfortable as long as you put a cushion on top of the plate. You didn't even know you were on it.

On the days I wasn't flying, I operated the Fire Direction Center. The duties there were quite different. At the center, you did all the calculations, and you were in communication with all the Marines who were out on patrol. Let's say a patrol saw some Viet Cong. They would call in to the center, saying, *"Fire mission!"* and, *"Azimuth!"* The azimuth is a degree you're looking at. Instead of 360 degrees you had 6,400 mils. You didn't know where you were, but you could put this compass up and tell how you are looking at the target: *"I don't know where I am, but I can see the target, and I'm going to give you approximate coordinates. I'm looking at the landmarks around."* And I said, *"Fire mission! Azimuth 3200. Coordinates 876430. Fuse: VT,"* meaning variable time fuse so that before the round hits, it explodes and throws the shrapnel, or *"Willy Peter,"* white phosphorus, which burned fiercely; we also used contact fuses or delayed fuses.

So the gunners sent a round out, and I was back in the Fire Direction Center, and we put a pin on a map for the coordinates. The gunners fired the center two guns of the battery, which put out about 200x100 meters of shrapnel. If it missed the target, the artillery observer might say right 400, drop 200, and fire another two rounds. If you dropped 200, the impact was on the other side. When I got to drop 50, you *"fired for effect"* — shoot as much as you can until ordered to stop. So that's how the guns walked in rounds until they hit the target. We did that all night and day, three shifts. Now when you are in the air, like I was, I could see the guns, I could see the target, and adjusted them along the target line — the line on which the gun was aimed. So when I said, *"Left 200,"* it meant left 200 meters off the current gun target line.

For eight hours a day, I had a fire direction shift. Occasionally, I went out as a forward observer with an infantry company where I was the artillery officer that adjusted fire. As a forward observer, it was like I was a part of the infantry company, and I was the artillery officer. I didn't operate the radio; I had a radioman to do that. If the infantry unit either saw Viet Cong or came under attack, the troops wanted artillery cover or an airstrike. So I computed the strike coordinates and had it called in. This was not very often; most of the time, I was an aerial observer.

Functioning through fear

I can't say if it was riskier as the forward observer or the aerial observer. I don't know. Shoot! I was scared; don't get me wrong. But I was able to function with fear. The Marine Corps taught you to do that. You were so intent on what you were doing that you lost track of being afraid. Then after the action was over, you reflected on it, and the danger you were in hits you.

Getting through the harrowing experiences made a team stronger. I will tell you about a bullet that missed me by inches. I was on a mission in a helicopter and several bullets penetrated the aircraft. It passed through the cabin and cut the radio cord off the back of my helmet. The pilot flying the chopper kept radioing me and didn't hear any response. He was worried that I had been shot because I wasn't answering. Bullets were hitting us. It was ping … ping! Ping-ping! I would describe it as the sound of rocks thrown at a dishpan. The VC had pinned down an infantry unit, and my job was to find the VC and have artillery blow the hell out of them. So we went up to 1,500 feet and looked around. I couldn't find them. Then we made a low pass, about 50 feet off the ground, and all of a sudden, I saw the enemy in *"black pajamas"* running around. That's when they started shooting at our aircraft.

Even though they shot up the aircraft so badly, we landed safely. Only one of the pilots got hit — a bullet went through the windshield and he got some glass in his cheek. He received the Purple Heart medal, while I just got my radio cord shot off. I had been looking down, but if I had had my head up, the bullet would've gone right through my ear. I'm not trying to be melodramatic; that's just the way it was.

When we were flying, we normally flew out of small arms range at 1,500 feet. But I flew below that a hell of a lot of times. Pilots account for what is called relative motion. If you're flying at, say, 50 feet, the enemy can't follow you very well; you go by so fast that they can't track you. It's either 1,500 feet or you're at treetop level. Because of the relative speed, the enemy can't train their guns fast enough generally to get on target. But if you're up at 500 feet, you're a sitting duck, you see? You're just floating along up there within range of small arms fire. Today, in Afghanistan, drones do what I did because the enemy can now shoot you down pretty easily.

Sometimes these huge B-52s flew over and dropped bombs, just blowing everything to hell. Then we would drop down to see what damage was done. Usually it just consisted of blown-up trees. Anyway, the dangerous situation for AOs then was when you were not flying at 1,500 feet. At least, at that time, surface-to-air missiles didn't exist, but when you descended, if you didn't know where the enemy troops were, they didn't want to expose their position. Once you spotted them and knew where they were, then they tried to shoot you down. So when you dropped to treetop level, man, it was always a hairy situation because they were trying to blow you out of the sky. It was a regular cat-and-mouse game.

One night, we were at the officers club we made — the Boom Boom Club, we christened it. It was a tent, and we got bomb racks from the airbase, put cement in them and made barstools. We made the bar out of bamboo. Finally, we scrounged up some beverages, and we played cards. It was a safe position. The colonel in charge of our unit, a full-bird colonel (the highest rank of colonel), loved to play bridge. We were playing a few games, and all of a sudden, some rounds started landing in the compound. The colonel ordered, *"Put your hands down. Don't disturb your hands."* So we put our cards down right where we were and went to investigate. A bunch of Viet Cong sappers were attacking the Chu Lai airfield, blowing up planes. Sappers were soldiers who were trained in explosives and infiltration. I spotted these guys running around the airstrip. I could see burning red fire apparently from mortar rounds that landed in the camp. The sappers had gone in the water inlet next to camp, breathed underwater through reeds until it got dark and then came out to attack. We had this fancy Army radar and tried to track where we thought the mortar rounds were coming from so we could shoot them. It turns out, we were doing all these calculations, but it was direct fire. It was VC who had slipped through the lines and were firing bazookas in our camp! So anyway, to make a long story short, it wasn't as bad as it could have been, though I think they got a couple of planes and some Marines.

When the firefight was over, we went back to the tent, and the colonel said, *"All right, let's pick up your hand and finish the game!"* I'll never forget that!

Time for some R&R

I only saw my wife, Barbara, one time in that year. You get rest and relaxation after four or five months, and you went to Thailand or Okinawa. In my case, I went to Okinawa. Today, everyone has a cell phone, but in those days, communication was very difficult. To call someone you had to radio a shortwave ham radio operator on the West Coast who could phone your wife and patch the phone call to the radio call. You had to say *"over"* and so on when you finished your sentence, and it was really difficult. I just told Barbara to be at Okinawa at a certain time. I didn't know if she was coming until I got there.

As I waited to leave, I sat on a sand dune at the Chu Lai airstrip. The planes were six hours late. They were bombing up north and were supposed to pick up those of us going on leave to take us to Okinawa. They finally showed up, but because of radio silence, we didn't know when the planes were coming. I landed on the island, and I checked if there were any messages for Lt. Mixon. I was in deep suspense. This guy says, *"Hmm. Hmm."* And I am waiting. *"Um, your wife's at the Tokyu Hotel,"* or something like that. Off I went. Anyway we had a really good time, and I bought a Porsche from Cars International. It would be waiting for me in San Francisco when my tour was up. I bought Barbara some fine quality Mikimoto pearls. I spent every dollar I had. I figured I wasn't going to make it. I thought, *"Shoot, I've got to go back into combat for another six months. There's no way I'm going to get out of Vietnam alive."*

So we spent all this money! The car was a brand-new Porsche 912. It had a new body style, and the salesman took me out to give me a demonstration on an abandoned airfield. He said, *"Let me show you what this car will do."* Zoom! It was scarier than Vietnam, I'm telling you. I mean you talk about speed ... my face was glued to the car windshield.

Anyway, the time came when I had to go back to Vietnam. I said goodbye to Barbara. We were crying. We kissed and all that. I reported to the plane to go to the base. I said to the sergeant, *"I've got orders that I'm supposed to be on this plane today."* He said, *"I can't get you on, lieutenant, we're backed up. Maybe tomorrow."* *"Well, my orders say I'm supposed to be on that plane today."* He said, *"Lieutenant, I've got more screwed-up Marines on this island than … I am still trying to find them and get them out of the brig."* They had been in combat and were now living it up. He said, *"I'll get you on this plane if you insist. But, officially, I can't get you on the plane until tomorrow."* He didn't have to tell me a third time. I called Barbara and luckily she wasn't planning to leave for another day. We had another day together, and it was a lot of fun.

The next day, I flew back to my base — here I was, leaving Okinawa and landing back in Vietnam the same day. My cohorts said, *"Hey, Mixon. It's your turn to fly. The helicopter is going to be here in an hour, get your gear on."* So that afternoon, I was back flying combat missions after being in Okinawa that morning. It was a peculiar feeling that it could happen so fast.

Another contrast that struck me occurred in the early part of the war when we were flying around Da Nang. You could see the French homes with people actually sunbathing by their swimming pools — and we were out there shooting at each other, and people were getting killed, and here are the French just relaxing. It was kind of jaw-dropping. They had a treaty with the Vietnamese. The Vietnamese didn't bother them, and the French just lived a fairly normal life.

Mixon for the defense

There were some times in Vietnam when I didn't have much to do intellectually so I started studying the judicial manuals. I decided to defend Marines who had been accused of infractions such as sleeping on post. The Marine Corps really took this seriously. The best defense I had was reasonable doubt — and to my credit, I got some guilty people off.

One day I was defending a guy accused of sleeping at his post during wartime conditions. That's a bad, bad thing. But you're there all night, you're sitting there and you tend to nod off. Usually the accused would say, *"No defense, I'm guilty."* The sentence then came down. ... But I decided to be a Johnnie Cochran, OJ's famous lawyer, who if he couldn't dazzle them with his logic, he would dazzle them with his drama.

Because the court thought I would enter a routine guilty plea, I'd say, *"Not guilty."* Then I start my arguments. *"Now, now you claim you caught Cpl. So-and-so sleeping on post."* I said, *"How do you know?"* He said, *"I called his name and he didn't answer."* I said, *"Was it dark?" "Yeah." "Did you see his eyes?" "No." "How do you know he was asleep? How do you know he wasn't concentrating on something?"* I created enough doubt, that my *"clients"* did not get convicted. Pretty soon, the word got around. Several Marines asked for Lt. Mixon to defend them.

Anyway, I won cases and the colonel called me in. I was standing there, and he said, *"Lieutenant, have you had a good time? You've done a really good job defending these Marines. I want to compliment you on defending these Marines. You've done a great job." "Thank you, sir,"* I said. *"But you aren't ever going to defend one again. I'm putting you on the other side." "Yes, sir,"* I said. He assigned me to prosecute the cases! But I lost interest after that. I didn't want to send Marines to the brig as a prisoner. I mean they were up all night, shoot, they were tired and sleepless.

Fighting the good fight

Since I didn't fly the aircraft used for aerial observer missions, I was very particular about who was my pilot. To some extent you could request a certain pilot. I tried to do the best I could picking out a guy I thought was going to make it. I want to tell you about two incidents. First, there was a guy who nobody liked to fly with. He was an Army captain, a mustang, and he flew completely around a target, against standard procedures.

You're never supposed to fly in the line of fire. You fly in semicircles back and forth. This idiot flew around the target like a circle. I finally said to him, *"Captain, would you mind flying to either side? The rounds are hitting all below us."*

He said, *"Lieutenant, there are too damn many things to worry about in this war than worrying about getting hit by an artillery round."*

He just kept flying around the target. By the way, he's still alive — he made it out. I went to his Army unit's recent reunion. I had not seen him since 1965.

In the second incident, I requested a pilot who I thought was the best one. Well, he later had a mid-air collision with a South Vietnamese pilot and died. I guess I could have, too.

I did fire a weapon once. Officers usually don't. I had been out flying on a mission with Army pilot Daryl McAllister for two or three hours. We were flying back really low because it was very foggy. We were following Highway 1, and all of a sudden, we came upon some VC, they were sitting on a bridge, dangling their legs over the edge and their weapons were right beside them. They were kind of lollygagging, just screwing off, talking. We banked around, I had an AR-15 semiautomatic rifle, and I just sprayed the area. They tried to run into the bushes. Daryl claimed I got three. I don't know, but we certainly ruined their day.

I've often said, *"I didn't mind shooting people."* You know, when you are in war conditions, you don't think of the enemy as human. They are going to kill you. It's kill or be killed. You kill someone, and sometimes, you find a picture in their pocket of their family, it makes you feel kind of lousy. But you are so scared that you aren't able to care. I don't give a damn who you're talking about. If somebody's shooting at you, you are scared. Sometimes, you can't even function. You ask yourself, *"Are you still stable enough that you can concentrate?"* All this stuff about guys who are brave and they do great things — you know they are scared, but they do it anyhow.

When we weren't fighting the enemy, we were fighting the weather. Everything you have ever heard about monsoon season is true. It just rains and rains and rains and everything gets wet, wetter, wettest. I didn't have much in the way of possessions, just a cot and a box that I had made into a sort of chest of drawers. One night, our tent just fell over because the ground got so wet. Zoop! It was about 2 o'clock in the morning, and the rain was just flooding down so everything I had got wet. I was all wet. It wasn't cold, just wet. And, all of a sudden, my buddies and I just started laughing. It was crazy because here we were, in the middle of Vietnam, in the middle of the monsoon; it was raining on us at 2 o'clock in the morning — what else could happen to us?

That wasn't the last time I felt like asking that. One of the most frightening things happened to me and one of my best friends from Harvard, Dick Adams. He was stationed in Da Nang and was a helicopter pilot. We hadn't seen each other since we went to basic school (six months in Quantico) together. Well, the colonel sent me to Da Nang to negotiate for some supplies for our camp. Dick picked me up in his helicopter. I was going up to spend a couple of days; it was just a routine flight. We were on our way to Da Nang, two helicopters flying in formation like they did when in pairs.

All of a sudden we ran into the most hellacious storm I've ever been in — I mean lightning, thunder, wind and rain. Of course, the side door of the helicopter was open, so the rain was streaming in. I looked up and saw Dick's legs, and they were shaking. He lost the other helicopter's position. Then all of a sudden, the other helicopter came back the other way. Zoom! It was lost obviously. I was sitting in the belly of the aircraft and all I could think about was that we were going to go down somewhere between Chu Lai and Da Nang. I was going to be killed, the enemy would desecrate my body by cutting my balls off and stuffing them in my mouth, and there was no way I was going to get out of this alive.

Somehow we got through the storm and made it to Da Nang. It was a perfectly clear day there. We landed and we literally kissed the ground. On this trip, I also saw my high school friend and later my best man, Jim Harris. He was running a motor transport unit there. That night, we found our way into a poker game. After hours, a Marine's a Marine and you never pull rank. So we were in this lively poker game, I looked over at one of the guys, and I saw a star on his collar. It was Gen. Marion E. Carl, who was the commander of our unit from Hawaii and one of the most decorated Marines in World War II. He shot down more than 20 Japanese planes and was the first fighter ace in Marine Corps history. I had never met him, but I got to play poker with him! Sadly, he was murdered in 1998 in his home in Oregon when a druggie broke into his house, shot him with a shotgun and killed him. Can you imagine a guy who served in World War II, Korea and Vietnam, was the most-decorated Marine pilot and a record-setting test pilot — all that, and he lost his life at home in a burglary?

Anyway, I was successful in my mission. I was able to arrange for a shipment of supplies for my unit. We actually had dinner in Da Nang at a Vietnamese restaurant. It was fairly peaceful at that time.

Occasionally a grenade went off or something. The restaurant was influenced very much by French cooking. It was very good.

The largest mission I was ever involved in actually made the history books. I was in Operation Starlite in August 1965, the first major battle in Vietnam conducted by American troops. I was on station all day long; I went out in a Cessna L-19 reconnaissance aircraft. If we needed fuel, we flew back to the airfield, and then we went back out again. I could see the Marines running ... it was like the hedgerows in Normandy during World War II when the Germans defended them and they were nearly impenetrable. These VC were chasing our troops down the rows. But we wiped out a bunch of Charlies that day. You can't win a war by killing Asians, but we killed a lot more, several hundred, than the 50 Marines who died in Operation Starlite, I will tell you that. That battle was near Chu Lai on the Quang Ngai peninsula.

When we would have an operation, the AOs went to Quang Ngai. There was an airstrip there, a Vietnamese airstrip. They had nice quarters for the pilots and the AOs, There were Vietnamese officers there, and they actually had a club with refreshments. We dropped in to visit their tiny officers' club.

To relax a little, we always had happy hour on Fridays. We had it out in the jungle, too. We are able to scarf up a little booze and stuff and when the wives or girlfriends sent Vienna sausage or some canned food, we had that for hors d'oeuvres. I was late to one happy hour because I was flying, and my fellow officers said, *"Hey Mal, we left you some. We had happy hour, but we left you some food behind the bar."* I was hungry and thirsty so I went to grab a bite. Well, this one guy was married to a Mexican woman, and she sent him the hottest thing I had ever tasted. I opened a beer and I took a bite of this Mexican pepper. All of a sudden I thought I was going to die! Talk about hot! So that night, I took the can of hot peppers to my fire direction center team, and I gave them a lecture: *"Now you men are supposed to be tough. You're Marines. Now I've got something here that is a little hot. How many of you would like to try one?"* They all held up their hands. They didn't want to be a chicken. So I went around the room, and put one in each guy's mouth, and each one writhed, literally writhed, *"Argh!"* They were dropping off like flies. I finally got to this kid from Texas, and he ate a pepper. He was munching away like nothing was unusual, and he said, *"Lieutenant, can I have another one of those?"* We all laughed, all of us who could!

Bob Hope, Phyllis Diller and Ann-Margret came to entertain the troops for Hope's annual holiday tour while I was there. I was among the small percentage that actually got to see his show. We hadn't had any entertainment in several months. There was actually a minor firefight before he landed on the airstrip, but the show went on. Ann-Margret was a gorgeous gal and she wore a tight black outfit. She came on stage before these Marines who hadn't seen a woman in six months; she said how happy she was to be there and how proud she was of the Marines. Then she said, *"I would like to make love to every one of you!"* Of course, the crowd went nuts cheering!

You certainly had to admire Bob Hope — he had gone out to entertain troops during World War II and Korea, and at that time, he was in his mid-60s in Vietnam, still entertaining our troops.

Winding down

My 13 months in Vietnam, counting the month in Okinawa, went by fairly fast, but near the end of your tour, you definitely got a short-timer's attitude. I didn't want to go out on a mission. My tour was about up; I could get killed! My last week or two, there had been an infantry unit pinned down under an attack. The infantry unit's commanding officer, a colonel, wanted to put together a ragtag emergency company to go out and give them relief. They needed an artillery officer to go with them. The captain chose a particular lieutenant. I won't mention his name, but he was assigned to go on this mission. Well, he started faking that he was sick, and they asked me to replace him. There I was, only a week or two to go, and I had to go on this damn mission. So as we walked along the trail, there were bloody bandages in some places — and we had a little firefight, but it wasn't much, and the Marines finally got relief before it was too late for them.

It was a long mission. I didn't get back to base until 11 o'clock or midnight. It was really late. I remember I walked in the tent, and I grabbed the *"sick"* lieutenant by the throat, and said, *"You're nothing but a f-----g coward. You know it and I know it. And I'm going to see you someday, and when you look at me, I want you to know that I think you are a coward."* The guys all pulled me off and wouldn't let me hurt him. I was about ready to kill the son of a bitch.

After I got out of Vietnam, I was in Philadelphia working as a salesman. I was at a restaurant, and guess what? He walked in. And I said, *"Hi, (his name),"* and he said, *"Hi, Mal,"* and just walked on by. I didn't want to talk to him. But he knew what I thought. He has to live with that his whole life. I'm sure he thinks about it — he must. But anyway, that was a story about the short-timer's attitude. I didn't want to go on the patrol either, but I was told to do it by my commanding officer, so I did. The other guy was about to finish his tour of duty, too, but he was chosen originally, not me. That's the point.

I remember the night I left Vietnam. I got so sick from celebrating, and I was so screwed up. I flew to Okinawa for a few days to recover before I picked up Barbara in Hawaii. The next day I quit smoking. I didn't want a cigarette; that's how sick I was.

For my service, I earned several Air Medals with Oak Leaf Cluster and Navy Commendation Medal with Combat *"V,"* honoring *"exceptional valorous actions"* in combat. I left Vietnam as a first lieutenant and was promoted to captain after serving in the reserves afterward.

I picked up Barbara in Hawaii, and we flew back to the mainland together. We went to Berkeley to see Barbara's friend and have dinner. I was very much in a kind of culture withdrawal. I had come out of Vietnam, but my mind was still there. Hell, I hadn't eaten on a tablecloth or much of anything for so long, and I thought, *"God, I'm sure they're going to ask me a lot of questions about Vietnam."* They didn't ask one question. I was sitting there and my mind was on Vietnam and they were talking about the trees or flowers or this or that. It was just like Vietnam didn't happen. The attitude of these people was, *"Oh, you were kind of unlucky. You had to go to Vietnam, huh?"* We were unappreciated. Sentiment against the war was starting to rise at that time and people were treating returning troops either indifferently or even as criminals. I couldn't understand it.

You see, after World War II, the returning Marines and soldiers were seen as heroes, my father among them. When they came home, they were greeted with parades and by cheering crowds. Not us. This time, the attitude of many American people was you weren't a hero; you were stupid.

But I never let it affect me. I just didn't talk about the war much. It was only a few years ago that I got my medals and my citation out to display them and talked about the war. I think The Vietnam Veterans Memorial Wall changed people's attitudes about Vietnam a little bit. It personalized it. The names on the wall are in the order that they were killed. The ones I knew who were killed are on the first few stones. I've seen their names and remember them all.

Aftermath

I had a Greek body — I was so fit when I left Vietnam, I am pretty proud to admit. I didn't have an ounce of fat on me. There hadn't been much to eat in Vietnam, and what there was turned out to be lousy food — ham and lima beans or other canned goods. I didn't eat that much, so I was pretty trim. As soon as I got home and quit worrying about combat, I started eating. Pretty soon those nice tailored suits I bought in Okinawa on the way home didn't fit me at all. Once while I was wearing a suit and bending down, I split my pants down the entire seam.

Some people ask me if I had post-traumatic stress disorder, PTSD. I don't know if I had it, but I was troubled by two things after the war. I received the rifle and pistol expert badge, so I was a very good shot, but I never had to use my weapon other than when I shot at those VC on the bridge. As an officer, I carried a .45-caliber pistol. I never used the damn thing. I still have one that I bought after the war for $25. Talk about eccentricities, I wanted that .45 near me at nights. It was kind of crazy, but I thought somebody might break into the house. I'm sure the weapon just gave me a sense of security.

One night when we lived in Cleveland Heights, my dog started barking. I got my .45 out and I said to Barbara, *"I think somebody's trying to break into the house."* Barbara said the dog was probably just barking at cars. Well, I didn't go downstairs to check it out. The next morning I went downstairs and found the window was open, and Barbara's purse was dumped out near the car outside.

The burglar must have been startled by the dog and took off. I probably would have shot him and asked questions later, but I didn't go downstairs. The whole thing was kind of freaky.

The other unusual thing was that for several years, I didn't want to fly on an airplane — any airplane. It would have reminded me of Vietnam. I just didn't like being in a plane. I got over it, but it took a while, as I had to put my mind to it. It was kind of crazy. But compared to what a lot of other guys had coming back, if that's all I had, that was nothing.

This next story just goes to show how strange coincidences can be. Gen. Nguyen Cao Ky, the premier of South Vietnam, landed at Chu Lai one time, and I got to shake his hand. He was the stylish guy with designer sunglasses and a mustache, and he often dressed in black with a scarf. A few years ago, I was in Las Vegas and this Asian guy walked by. I was with my lawyer, and I said to him, *"That guy looks like Premier Ky."* So my lawyer said, *"Why don't you go over and say, 'Hello, Premier Ky'?"* I said, *"Well, I'm not sure it's him, but it certainly looks like him."* So I didn't think anything more of it.

Later on that afternoon, I was gambling at the casino, and left the craps table to play the one-armed bandit or something else and here came this same guy walking back in. This must have been fate. I said, *"Are you Premier Ky?"* He said, *"Yes, I am."* I told him who I was and that I had served in Vietnam. We talked for about an hour. He said, *"I really appreciate what you did for my country, and I'm sorry we lost the country."* We reminisced some more about Vietnam and I asked him what he was doing. He said he was teaching school in California, and had come out to Las Vegas for something or other. But I thought that was an amazing coincidence.

I've been to Vietnam, and I've always said, the most important thing I got out of Vietnam was my ass. That's true, because it was a wasted war. There were 58,000 Americans who died. Of course, as a young man, I thought I was doing my duty for my country. I couldn't imagine going through life without having been in combat. That's how gung-ho I was. I couldn't be a man unless I had been in uniform and under fire. But once I got under fire, that's all I needed, you know. Then you think you're invincible, that it can't happen to you.

In a tent in Chu Lai, I had typed out my application for the Harvard Business School. I was thinking of going into business. ...

*My dad, Chief Yeoman Aaron Malachi
Mixon Jr. and me, Aaron Malachi Mixon
III, circa 1943 during World War II,
Spiro, Okla.*

About 6 years old, wearing bib overalls.

In my cowboy outfit.

Wearing my baseball uniform as a teen.

Riding my horse Scout in Spiro, Okla.

My boyhood home on Mixon Hill, Spiro, Okla. (2012 photo).

After being commissioned lieutenant in the U.S. Marine Corps, early 1960s.

In full dress Marine uniform, with Barbara at my side.

With Barbara during our early days as a couple.

Kneeling by a signpost in Vietnam.

In the FDC (fire direction center) where we made artillery calculations.

By a supply tent in Vietnam.

Boarding a jet, summer 1960, for training in Corpus Christi, Texas.

Chapter 4: Getting my MBA

While I was sitting in that tent in Chu Lai, thinking about what was ahead for me, I made a conclusion. For a long time while I was in Vietnam, I didn't know for sure what to pursue for a career. I wanted to go to business school, to law school or maybe medical school. Law school seemed too narrow of a profession. Medical school (shades of my grandfather) seemed like it took too long, six to eight years of school. Business school was only two years and offered a lot of flexibility. So the decision was obvious.

I applied to Harvard, Columbia, Pennsylvania and Stanford. I got accepted by the first three. Anyway, the choice was easy — I went back to Harvard to get my MBA. I've often felt that I was much more settled down compared to when I went to Harvard as an undergraduate. There were a lot of fun things to do the first time around. I was chasing girls, athletics, working a job and everything. I think I could have been a better student and was interested in getting acceptable grades, but I was unwilling to make the commitment to be a really dedicated student. However, when I went to the business school, I was a very serious student. I had just served in Vietnam, and I knew

I had to join the workforce. So I worked pretty hard, and I wasn't dating — I was married after all — and I did a lot better academically than I had done as an undergraduate.

The pain of writing papers

The thing I remember most about business school was that in one class, every other Friday, we had to start working on a paper due the next morning. It was called a Written Analysis of Cases, or a WAC. You were given a case to analyze and you developed a solution. The practice dates back to the early 1900s. The HBS faculty felt first-year marketing course students should be assigned to write WACs regularly on a short deadline. So, over the years, it became a big tradition. You generally stayed up all night Friday night doing the WAC and turned it in by 8 o'clock the next morning.

The godfather of the WAC was HBS professor Thomas J.C. Raymond. He maintained that, by writing the papers, it would help a student learn the skills to go out in the real world and in effect put together his own case. He figured that when a student's schooling was over, no one would just hand him a case ready to analyze and the student needed the know-how.

But this assignment's charm, if you'd call it that, was that you had to drop the WAC down a chute at the west end of Baker Library before the deadline. You had to submit the case on time or the receptacle box was pulled away and your WAC fell on the floor — and you got an *"unsatisfactory performance."* The pressure was intense and often you'd see students running to the chute to beat the clock. There would be a crowd gathered, and they'd cheer them on.

The WAC was a bitch because you were tired, you'd studied all week, you had gone to school all week, and then you had to do this WAC. One other thing that I remember in connection with it was that my father insisted I take typing when I was a kid in Spiro. So I learned to type — not a one-finger kind of typing. I mean I could really type — 60 words a minute — and believe me, I spent hours doing WACs — and Barbara didn't have to type for me.

When I think about it, I really enjoyed Harvard Business School. I learned a lot because I really knew very little about business. I loved my courses. I recall that Charlie Williams taught finance; Jay Lorsch, human behavior in organizations; Milt Brown, marketing. For me, it was quite a big step compared to those who grew up in business environments with their fathers.

Interestingly, the class voted me to be the first ombudsman — as the interface with the dean on things they wanted input on throughout the school. I mean we had some real issues like what was the content of the vending machines — important matters like that. They figured I was tough enough to stand up for their rights. It was fun.

It was my only foray into elected office. I wouldn't take a political job if they gave it to me. That's how I feel about it. When I was a boy, I used to think politicians were so much smarter than me … brilliant people, you know, congressmen, senators. Now I know they are not as smart as we are (there are a few exceptions). Who would take the damn job? They just give TV sound bites all the time, they don't know anything about anything much, and if my good friend Ohio Gov. John Kasich called me tomorrow and told me the U.S. senator from Ohio dropped dead and he wanted to appoint me senator, I'd tell him get somebody else. I have no ambition to go into politics.

Getting good grades and offers

I fulfilled my goal to get good grades. I graduated with distinction, which put me in the top 50 of the 600 students. I had started job hunting and received several offers. I remember sitting on the couch with Barbara and trying to decide among the offers. Goldman Sachs in New York made an offer. There was one from the Industrial National Bank of Rhode Island, which was for $14,000 annual salary. Harris Intertype of Cleveland offered me a job for $13,500. We agonized over that $500 difference. I decided that Barbara would be happier in her hometown of Cleveland, so that's why I came to Cleveland. I had no family or connections in the area, but at that time, there were a lot of Harvard guys who worked for Harris Intertype. There was nothing to do in Spiro as far as employment, obviously. So as I've always said, I became a kind of a reverse carpetbagger, a Southern boy who ended up in the North.

I learned more about leadership in the Marine Corps than I learned at Harvard. I've said that many times. In those days, they didn't teach leadership as a class. You may think you're academically bright enough to lead, but I've known a lot of bright people who aren't good leaders. They're smart, but they don't know how people are. They don't know how people react. I know people who can say different words and arrive at the same point, but say it in a way that people want to follow you. A reporter once called me and said Harvard Business School was going to teach a course on ethics and asked me what I thought about it. I said, *"Well, if you don't have ethics by now — from your minister, your parents or your coach — you probably don't have any so I don't know how you're going to teach them, except maybe situational ethics."*

When I was a child in Spiro, my teachers never spoke to me about owning or starting a business. I knew absolutely nothing about how to start or run a business. It was always, *"Who are you going to work for?"* or what I wanted to be. It was never, *"Do you know how to start up or run a business with only a little money?"* The schools never brought into my classroom anyone who taught me anything about business until I entered HBS. The closest I ever came to running a business was my childhood lemonade stand in Idabel, Okla., at my Aunt Eva Jane's house.

This situation really needs to change in America; we have to change the mindset among those teaching our youngsters. The lower grades are not too early for students to learn entrepreneurship.

Chapter 5: Bearding the Lion

My first position after graduating from Harvard Business School was as assistant controller of the Seybold Division of Harris Intertype Corp. This was about a $60 million division, and at that time, it made sheet-fed lithographic color printing presses. The quality was so outstanding that many top publications used the presses; the Harris presses even printed the centerfold of *Playboy* at the time.

Besides that bit of trivia, I realize that my Harris experience was one of the most important of my career. If I hadn't worked for Harris, I wouldn't have met E.P. *"Pat"* Nalley. He was one of the most influential people in my career. Pat taught me a lot about sales. He was the best salesman I ever met.

It all began when I sat down in the Harris cafeteria one day with this man who happened to be Pat Nalley. He was the vice president of sales for the division. He said to me, *"How do you like your job? I said, "Not worth a s---. I've been here six months, and I hate it. I am really disappointed."*

I was really enthusiastic about trying to find problems and things that should be repaired. So my boss called me in and said, *"The fact is, I have enough problems with my boss. I don't need to tell him about any more problems."* That attitude kind of demoralized me. Here was a guy who didn't want to be the best, didn't want to pursue excellence and who was telling me, *"Don't find me any more problems. I have enough already."* When I started this job, some folks told me that this boss was weak and needed some *"shoring up."* He really didn't want any help. He was scared and insecure. He was much older than me, and I was only 28.

Pat alerted me to something very promising. *"We are not allowed to pirate young people from other departments, but there is going to be a notice going up that I am looking for an assistant marketing person,"* he said. *"Every department is required to tell other department heads that this job is available. If you are interested, tell your boss and you can apply for the job."* So the notice was posted on the board. My boss called me and told me about the marketing position. *"I'm sure you're not interested, but I have to tell you about it,"* he said. *"Oh, I am interested!"* I replied.

Well, I was offered the position and I took it. I didn't even have an office — just a desk in the hallway. My new boss was another Harvard guy who was at least 10 or 15 years older than me, and he was very capable. There was no job description. There wasn't anything, and I began to go around to people in Pat Nalley's department and ask what I could do for them — everything anybody didn't want to do or didn't have an idea how to do it. So I created my own job. Pretty soon people were saying, *"Shoot, if you want to get that problem solved, talk to Mal!"*

One example: At that time, I still knew how to do FORTRAN computer programming. Pat had a personal real estate problem, and he didn't know what to do about it. I offered my help, wrote a FORTRAN program on the computer and printed out three or four alternatives. I did it in about an hour. Pat was so amazed that I was able to show depreciation, cash flow and everything that he took an immediate liking to me.

Learning from a pro

At that time, the sales effort was very dominant at Harris. The printing presses were expensive capital equipment, selling from $15,000 to $1 million each. I decided that I wanted to take on sales and have a territory. Most MBAs didn't want to be in sales because, in my opinion, it is too easy to measure if you succeed or fail. You know there is no way around it, and they are insecure about going into sales. Marketing was a safer field to choose. It turned out that I was very good at sales, and I made a lot of money selling.

My sales position was a salary-plus-commission job, so I was only limited by my ability and imagination. Here again, it was a new challenge for me, and I was up to meeting it. I had a territory that went from Cleveland as far south as Columbus, Ohio. One time I went to a motel in Columbus and, to prepare for my sales calls, I circled on a map everywhere I wanted to go. Then I would draw the shortest distance to each of them so I would end up back at the hotel at quitting time. Anyway, I talked to this one printer about getting a new press. His shop was rather disheveled, and his bottom line was that he couldn't fit the press in his place, so he didn't buy. Well, undaunted, I went back to my motel that night, and I drew up a redesign for his printing shop for him, putting the equipment in all different places. I went back the next morning and asked him, *"If I were to show you how you could re-layout this plant and fit this press in, would you buy it?"* He said he might. So I took all these templates out and showed him what I did, he was convinced, and I sold him the press. That's taking customer service to the next level, I would say.

Another time, Pat was trying to teach me a few things, so he sent me to this shop in New York's printing district, which was called Printers' Alley. It was just printer after printer after printer there. So I walked into this big printer's office, and he said, *"What the f--- do you want, kid?"* Those were the first words out of his mouth. So I shot back, *"I want to sell you a f----g printing press."* He said, *"Good, I want to buy one."* I mean, bang, bang, bang. Then I made the mistake of giving him my best price right away. He chiseled and chiseled and chiseled at the price for about the next three months. He kept calling me. He wanted the press, but he wanted a better price. So I went there again to try to close this damn order, and the printer said to me, *"Young man, don't ever, ever, EVER give your best price the first time out of the chute. You take all the fun out of negotiating."*

Well, he eventually purchased a press, but I learned something from that. By offering my best price, I left no room to negotiate. The customer naturally assumes your first offer isn't likely your best. You know, it's in people's DNA that they want to negotiate. Buyers want to feel they persuaded the sales rep to go down from his original offer. I learned to put in some wiggle room as far as price and terms. I also had to have some fundamental issues in the deal that were flexible. And I needed to have some *"throwaway"* issues that I really didn't care about — but could be conceded as part of the deal.

Pat then sent me to a printer in Columbus, Georgia. He told me, *"Mal, don't talk business with this man for about two or three hours. Talk about quail hunting, riding horses, and then eventually, he'll bring up that he wants to buy a press."* So I was thinking and contrasting this to the New York call — which took about 30 seconds to get the sale — to this one down in southern Georgia where the pace is slow and easy. Well, this guy was a hallmark printer, a really great craftsman, so he was an important customer. Pat told me, *"At the very end of your sales pitch, he will say he wants to trade in his old used press. He doesn't use it anymore, but he wants to get value for each trade-in. So save a little something for the trade."* I said, *"OK, I will."*

I went to see him, and we talked about everything. It was like we were just visiting, and he was trying to determine if he liked me or not. I liked to visit; if you meet an interesting guy, I can talk, you know, shoot the breeze. Every good salesman has got to have the gift of gab. This man was a Harris printer so he wasn't going to buy anything else. Eventually, he came around to talking about the press. I had saved enough to give him a trade-in allowance. It was such an old press that Harris never even took it back. They just left it on the premises. So I had another sale to my credit. I tell this story to show how dissimilar it was like to sell in New York compared to the Deep South at that time.

I also learned a thing or two about collecting past-due payments. Pat once took me to New York where a printer had not made a final payment on his press. I think it was a $1 million press and he owed about $100,000 or $200,000. He claimed that there were quality problems. So we went to New York, and this press was humming along, running flat out. Pat took a service technician along with us, and he had this guy put on a white coat like a doctor, complete with a stethoscope. The technician went around this press listening with his stethoscope, placing it on the vital parts, listening here, listening there.

Finally, he said, *"Shut her down, Pat! There is something wrong with this press! Shut her down."* So Pat said, *"We are going to take the press out of here!"* Of course, if he had taken it out of there, the printer would have been shut down for six months. Finally, the printer said, *"Wait! Wait! Pat! I'll pay!"* That was a lesson in collections. Pat had orchestrated this whole damn thing with the service guy and the stethoscope. His job as vice president of sales also involved collections, and that was his version of how he was going to collect the money. It worked like a charm.

To this day, I've always said you don't really get an order until you ship the product and then collect. You've got to collect. I devised an incentive system when I was working at one of my next jobs. The sales representatives didn't get paid their full commission until they collected the full amount. We held back the commission until then, and it really worked. It forced the sale reps to be interested in collecting the amount due.

One of the nice things about selling expensive printing presses was that even though I was a novice young salesman, I got to throw my sales pitch to the company president. As it was an important decision, the president didn't delegate it to subordinates. I met many business leaders that way.

Earning promotions

Success was coming my way, and I went from salesman to district manager to regional manager of sales. During that time, the company decided to consolidate the sales districts from 12 to six. While some people had to be let go, I was a survivor, stationed out of Atlanta with a territory that took in the Atlanta area all the way to New Orleans. I also inherited the Baltimore office in the shakeup. My new territory took in Philadelphia, Baltimore, Washington, Maryland — the whole East Coast. I had moved to Atlanta, I was really doing well, and I was earning a lot of money.

One day, Pat called me in to his office, and told me about an opening for director of marketing. He wanted me to take it, but it was for less money than I was making because I was earning sales incentives. After we had a long discussion, I told him, *"Gee, it sounds really interesting. I'd like to have the job. Now I can be a leader to the salesmen since I will not be spouting theory about sales — I've been there. Since I now know how to sell, when I talk, I think they would listen."*

I got offered the job, and since it would have been a cut in my compensation, I said I was not going to take a job for less money. Pat said, *"Well, hell, I wouldn't either!"* So Pat talked to his superior and came back and told me they would give me what I wanted.

I never looked back with any disappointment at my Harris experience. I got into an area I really liked — selling. I have always been a very external person, and I like going out and talking with customers. I also love to develop products. I spent a lot of time in the field, and I know a lot of customers. I loved selling, and I feel that selling taught me something that can't be taken away. It's a skill set that's really important. You sell to customers, you sell your bank to lend you money, and you sell people on joining your company. Even more important is that you learn about your company when you are selling. You can sit in an office and talk yourself into anything. But if you go out and talk to customers, they will tell you how you're doing — and they're never happy, it seems. They want it smaller, lighter, for less money or faster. I don't mean that critically; we are all that way. I learned that is just the nature of the customer.

CT scanners and TCB

I soon became the head of computerized tomography scanner marketing at Ohio-Nuclear, a subsidiary of Technicare Corp., which specialized in medical diagnostic-imaging equipment.

I'm not bragging, but I think I was and am a pretty good salesman — and I'd like to talk about a few tricks I find useful in my sales career. When I was at Ohio-Nuclear/Technicare, we got a new company jet. During the Christmas season once, I told my men that I wanted to fly everywhere we were about to lose a scanner order and keep those customers. CT scanners at that time were selling for $500,000.

I flew to New Orleans, Baton Rouge and all over, and I ended up at a North Carolina hospital where I was about to lose the order. At that time and very selectively, a competitor was discounting $50,000 off the price of a scanner but only when the competitor's salesmen thought they were about to lose the order. This competitor would go to $450,000 — everywhere else they sold at full list price; nothing was normally discounted.

I was making my call at the hospital, and I noticed on the president's desk a check for $50,000, the down payment on the competitor's scanner. A good salesman can read upside down, you see. Till then, the hospital had all Ohio-Nuclear equipment so we weren't totally foreign to them. I went through all my pitches to tell them why my scanner was better than the competitor's. He finally said, *"Mr. Mixon, we've made up our minds. We voted and we are going to buy the competitor's scanner. I thought I wouldn't send the order in until you came out and made your pitch, and I appreciate you flying all the way out here."*

I don't know why I did the next thing. *"You know, that's very nice of you,"* I said. *"I'd like to save you $50,000."* The guy said, *"What do you mean, save me $50,000?"* I said, *"Well, if you could call the competitor's office in Atlanta and tell them that Mal Mixon, the VP of marketing for Ohio-Nuclear is here, and you are trying to decide which scanner you want to choose. Ask him if $500,000 is his best and final quote. I think he will cut $50,000 off his price."* I had no idea what the competitor would do.

The hospital president did call the competitor's office, and over the phone, he reduced the price by $50,000. Well, in the South they are, shall we say, very strong on principal, honor and all that stuff. The president was really steaming he hadn't been given the lowest price. He called me back in his office and said, *"Mr. Mixon, you just got a scanner order."* I love to tell that story.

Back then, the advantages of having a company jet were enormous. We were flying around to wherever we needed while our competitors took commercial flights. They often weren't able to book flights while we flew into city after city. I told my team I wasn't interested in glad-handing — making a courtesy call and shaking the guy's hand for an order that we were going to get anyway. I wanted to go where we were not going to get a sale and try to turn the deal around. I think we got six or seven scanner orders that we would have lost.

It's no surprise that I got a thrill out of getting an order where somebody else couldn't or turning a bad situation around. A lot of people are scared of those kinds of situations. They don't want to do what salespeople call *"bearding the lion." "Bearding"* means you run in to cut the beard off the lion without the lion eating you to show that you are brave. I've always been that way ever since I started as a salesperson. I like to go where I can make a difference. I did my homework and knew my products, but the fun thing was that most of my selling was to fairly educated, top-level people and not some technocrat who doesn't appreciate economics or quality or that sort of thing.

Meeting J.B. Richey

Another important thing that happened to me at Ohio-Nuclear was that I met Joseph *"J.B."* Richey. He was the technical brains — he is the technical brains — behind Invacare. I can't fix a light switch, but I am very good at understanding what a customer wants, and J.B. is very good at designing it. The two of us got along really well together.

He had invented the first full-body CAT scanner. He's a brilliant guy. When we became partners, we used to plot what kind of business we're going to do. J.B. interviewed me when I first started at Ohio-Nuclear and he concluded, *"We are trying to hire a sales head, but frankly, I don't know why we need you."* I asked, *"What do you mean?"*

He replied, *"My product is so good, the orders just keep coming in. It sells itself."* So I said, *"Well, someday you may need a sales guy."*

Several years later, there was a company called AS&E, out of Boston. The company came up with a device that used a different way to scan. Their image was better than ours. I discovered this when I was making a call at a Catholic hospital, and the decision-makers there had an order for a scanner on the desk ready for me, but first, they said they had to run to Boston to see this company, AS&E. They wanted to look at the pictures, but said they would give me the order the next day.

As it was, I stuck around, but they decided on AS&E. They tore up my check, and I lost the order. AS&E had a better image than we did. We still kept getting lots of orders, but the handwriting was on the wall. I was talking with J.B. not long after, and he said, *"Mal, I don't understand it. This company's machine has better images than we have and yet we are getting all these orders."* I said, *"Well J.B., I've been burdened all my life by inferior engineers,"* and I just looked over with slight envy at AS&E's machine. Anyway, we kind of bonded. I think at that point he realized he did need me. I was good at sales, and he was good at engineering. When I later bought Invacare in 1979, J.B. stayed behind at Ohio-Nuclear. We couldn't afford two big salaries at Invacare. Not that I had a big salary; in fact, I took a cut. But when I could afford it about four years later, I brought J.B. over, and he started full-time at Invacare. It was one of my best moves ever.

While at Ohio-Nuclear, I was a very customer-focused guy. I thought I was so good at marketing and selling, but I was looking for a bigger challenge, with more responsibility. But management thought that was where I should stay, in sales. They weren't willing to give me a division. They weren't willing to make me a general manager. I was offered a big VP sales job with Johnson & Johnson who had just bought Technicare, but I would have had to move. I didn't want the job because I thought I was ready to be a general manager. It was time to part ways.

At that point I was just on the payroll, looking for a home. For about a year I was with MRI New Ventures trying to come up with some new things involving magnetic resonance scanning. I worked for a guy who decided he wanted to have somebody else in my job. So he put in this other guy in the job. They didn't fire me; they just moved me laterally. ... It really tore at me. What it told me was that they didn't think that highly of me. This one particular guy messed up my career aspirations, and nobody overruled him, which was kind of a shock, too.

So that led me to a conclusion — I finally said to myself, *"The only way I'm going to be a general manager is to buy a little company or something. I'd have to put myself in the job, rather than have somebody put me in a position."*

It was a period in my life when I was disappointed. I had worked my ass off, and I hadn't made any money. I kept questioning my life. I finally told Barbara that I would like to have a little thing that was my own. I didn't want to play politics in a big company, and I thought the whole Ohio-Nuclear thing was very political. Regardless, that caused me to look outward. If I had had a perfect career, I probably never would have become an entrepreneur. I was dealing with a career interruption, and although I wasn't fired, I had hit a wall, which was very upsetting to me. So I had to consider another path — and I probably would not have done that had I not been in this predicament.

Anyway, that led me to Invacare. I decided to take a risk — it really wasn't much of a risk even though I didn't know anything about wheelchairs. You know, it's a very funny thing. People see me as a risk-taker, but I don't see myself as one because I don't do stupid things. And I don't do what I don't think isn't going to work. Most things I've tried have worked. A risk-taker, to me, would be like shooting craps or betting on football. I like to do that on occasion, but I know the risk.

Barbara and Mal in the 1960s.

Feeding time for baby Elizabeth in late 1969.

112

images

Nov. - Dec. 1978

Vol. 2 No. 6

The Far East:
New markets for diagnostic imaging

Mal Mixon, in addition to his responsibilities as Vice President of Marketing for the Domestic CT operation, has assumed the responsibility for the sales and marketing activity in the Far East for all products manufactured by Ohio-Nuclear and Unirad. As the recently appointed Vice President, Far East Marketing, he manages an international distribution network that includes the Orient, Australia and New Zealand.

While many Ohio-Nuclear employees hear the term "international" applied to the company's marketing operations, few of them realize the awesome implications of that word. In one geographical area of this vast globe, the Far East, the marketing activity is also expanding.

"Japan, a country of about 125 million people -- about half our [population] size -- will buy probably 50 major CT units over the next year," said Mal Mixon in a recent interview. "In addition, many low cost 100 Series type scanners will be purchased."

Needless to say, ONI is competing with several other manufacturers for its market share of those sales.

Tracing out some history of the

continued

Mal Mixon

Photo by Pete Petterson

Article about my new position at Ohio-Nuclear, 1978.

..Malachi Mixon III

Mixon Heads Firm

A group of Cleveland area investors has purchased Invacare Corp., an Elyria wheelchair firm, from Technicare Corp.

The group includes Malachi Mixon III, 39, a former Technicare vice president who now is president and chief executive of Invacare. Mixon said the sale was for nearly $8 million in cash.

Mixon is a former three-sport athletic star at Spiro High School. He was born and reared in Spiro, graduating with the class of 1958. He holds a bachelor of arts degree from Harvard College and a master's degree in business administration from Harvard Business School. Malachi is the son of Mrs. Martha Mixon and the late Aaron M. Mixon, Jr., and the grandson of the late Dr. A. M. Mixon, pioneer area physician.

Invacare, with plants in Elyria and Lodi, employs about 350 persons who make wheelchairs and other patient aids including walking aids, lifts, commodes and traction equipment.

With annual sales of about $20 million, it is the second largest maker of wheelchairs after Everest & Jennings International of Los Angeles.

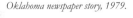

Oklahoma newspaper story, 1979.

With my mentor, E.P. "Pat" Nalley.

J.B. Richey and his Labrador retriever, Honey.

Standing before map of Europe to show Invacare's expansion there.

In my Invacare plant for the launch of Action sports wheelchair.

With my family and business associates opening trading on the NYSE for Invacare (IVC), June 25, 2000.

*At an Alaska scenic point
while on a fishing trip.*

*Fishing in Alaska with Joe Teague,
former Technicare CEO.
That's a sizable salmon.*

Chapter 6: Cancer

I tell you it came out of the blue — cancer. I was 37. I was giving serious thought to owning a company although I hadn't yet taken steps to buy Invacare. So there I was, married, with two children, a successful businessman living in Cleveland Heights — and a diagnosis of testicular cancer that knocked me on my ass.

It all started one day when I felt some heaviness. There was no pain. I thought I had better go to the doctor (my grandfather taught me well); maybe I had strained myself or something. My regular doctor was on vacation, so I picked an urologist out of the phone book and made an appointment. The doctor examined me and said, *"You've got a tumor."* I said, *"Oh, really? What are the chances that it is malignant?"* He said, *"About 98 percent."* I said, *"Judas Priest!"*

I immediately had thoughts of my mortality. My father had died of pancreatic cancer just seven years earlier. Everything seemed to come crashing down. My exam was on a Saturday, but I didn't sit around all weekend and mope about it. I went into action. I was concerned but not panicky. I called a friend who worked at the Cleveland Clinic, Ralph Alfidi, the head of radiology, at his home. He said, *"Mal, I will arrange for you to see another doctor; his name is Clarence Hewitt. He used to be at Walter Reed Army Medical Center and has done more surgeries for testicular cancer than any doctor in the United States. He's an expert,"* Ralph said. *"I will arrange for you to see him the first thing Monday morning, or if you want, I will call him and see if he is home today and you can see him at his house."* Of course, I said I would like to see him at his house. This is all on the same Saturday — I had been to the urologist in the morning, called Ralph, and now the specialist agreed to see me. And I didn't even have the pull of being on the board of the Cleveland Clinic at this point.

In kind of an odd coincidence, Dr. Hewitt lived in my old neighborhood of Shaker Heights, almost directly across the street from the first house I bought in the Cleveland area. I waited in his house for a few minutes, and then he examined me. He told me there were different types of tumors. The first type, seminoma, is very treatable. He said he would guess that mine was seminoma because of my age, but he didn't know for sure. He wouldn't know until he operated. *"I will make you my first patient Monday morning,"* he said.

The rest of Saturday and Sunday I was depressed and afraid. I was so scared — I just felt my life was over. I was saying to myself, *"Shoot, I got through Vietnam OK, and here I am just 37, and I am going to die of cancer. That doesn't seem right."* But I was manly about it; I mean I wasn't crying or anything. They say it's not unusual for a cancer patient to go through the same stages of grief as the bereaved do: denial, anger, bargaining, depression and acceptance. I went through them all very quickly.

On Monday morning, Dr. Hewitt operated and removed the tumor. It turned out to be a seminoma, which was a relief. I felt I had a good chance of beating this, but I was worried, about death, about my sex life and other things. They had given me some Demerol, a painkiller, and I felt like I was kind of in outer space. However, as the Demerol was wearing off, I got a phone call.

It was one of my old school teachers. I was immediately taken back in my mind to Spiro. *"Boy ... I hear you've had a rough day,"* he said. I replied, *"I have. They cut off my ball today." "I'm going to tell you something that only my mother and my wife know,"* he said. *"What's that?"* I asked. *"Mal, I was born with one ball. That's all I have,"* he said.

Of course this guy had several children and was everything a man ought to be. Anyway, that one telephone call really cheered me up. You can imagine, I had a lot these questions. ...

Shortly after the surgery, my secretary and the girls in the office devised a scheme. They came into my room; there were four or five of them, all cute girls. They sort of conjured up a trick they would pull on me. They turned on the charm and started caressing me and cooing to me, *"Mal, we are real sorry. We're all worried about you."* They were feeling my brow, rubbing my arm and my leg. I said, *"Please don't do that! It is going to hurt me too much! I'm already hurting!"* Anyway, it was a big joke.

I soon went back to work. Many of my colleagues did not know what had happened to me because I left work on a Friday. I think I missed only four days. For the follow-up care, I had to go through 18 radiation treatments in the upper body and 18 treatments in the lower left side. I think I had treatments three times a week, and almost to the hour after I had a treatment, I would throw up; that part was not fun. But I went to work through it all.

When I was receiving radiation, the head of radiation therapy was Dr. Tony Antunez. I was still working for Technicare, and one day while receiving treatment, he said, *"Mal, I need a scanner." "What the hell do you need a scanner for?"* He was talking about scanning cadavers so he could find cancer and other stuff. I got an old model scanner and was able to give it to him for his department. It was, in a way, my gesture of gratitude for the care I was receiving.

I knew cancer could come back, and if it were going to return, it usually came back in the first five years. Every time I went in for a blood test, I was scared that the cancer would return. Fortunately, it didn't, and I'm 72 now. It took me five years, the usual amount of time the doctors say, before I believed I was cured. But, at the time, I never told my bank, I never told investors and never told anyone other than Barbara about my cancer. I guess the people at Technicare knew about it. I didn't talk about it. That's how I wanted to deal with it then. Everyone works out his or her own feelings on it.

What I want to say is that your life is not going to go in a straight line. You are going to have setbacks. You've got to have strength to get through the tough times, not the easy times. Everyone can enjoy those. When you have a problem, you have to work your way through it. Cancer had a marked impact on my life. It made me a very somber guy. After the combination of combat and cancer, I wasn't very much afraid of anything. Many people get upset and fly off the handle about any little thing, and I'm sort of like, *"Let me tell you what to worry about."* I'm not saying that I'm a brave guy or anything, but the first time somebody shoots at you, it's very sobering. I went through that, and then I went through cancer, and I thought I was going to die of cancer. The feeling was very intense. But once I got through those two things, I said, *"Give me a break. Every business challenge is easy compared to them."*

Surviving cancer helped me with my life in terms of being able to face up to business problems. They're not real problems compared to those kinds of problems. I think beating cancer actually makes you a stronger person, more appreciative. It really puts the world in perspective. A lot of people complain about this or that. Well, what's the deal? Cancer made me say I'm going to enjoy life. I'm going to enjoy everything.

Chapter 7: The Amazing Invacare Story

I learned a lot after 11 years, working for four companies, especially Harris-Seybold and Technicare, and I decided I had just busted my butt. I was tired of making money for everybody but old Malachi, so I said, *"The next time I do this, I would like to do it for myself."*

At that point in my career, I was 39, people would say, *"Mal's a great sales marketing executive; I'm not sure if he's ready for general management yet."* I could've moved from Cleveland and pursued a sales marketing function for a large division of J&J. But I decided, after talking with my wife, I really would rather have something that was mine that I could run, and I thought I was ready to run a business.

My original partner and contemporary, J.B. Richey, and I decided we wanted to go into business together. He was a genius in engineering and product development. We both had been successful working for other companies but neither of us had accumulated much capital. Most of our discussions were held after work at the Ramada Inn on Rockside Road in Bedford Heights, Ohio, because it was convenient for both of us — and most importantly, it served free chicken wings in the lounge. They were good! We used to plot our moves to develop new companies.

Soon, we took a look at Invacare. Johnson & Johnson had acquired Technicare and had wanted to unload the Invacare division for three years. Invacare was a sleepy little company. As I say, I like to go where I can make a difference, and I wanted to turn it around. I thought I could take this thing and make something of it. And lo and behold, we made $1.4 million pretax the first year, but I'll get to that later.

Getting investors

Looking back, my first shot at owning a company almost didn't happen — for a number of reasons. It was difficult to get the financing. That's why I always say buying Invacare was harder than running Invacare. I literally only had my life savings of $10,000 to invest. The company was for sale for $7.8 million, and I've often told the story that all I needed was $7.79 million, and I had the company! There were some other potential buyers, and they already had tied up the support of major Cleveland banks. Interest rates were on the way up to 24 percent. I put my house and both cars in my wife's name, just in case everything fell apart. I said to myself, *"What is the worst thing that can happen to me? I'd lose $10,000. I'm only 39 years old, and I can get a job."*

I was successful in getting the investors I needed. Of everybody I presented the proposal to, half of them said yes. I met many of my early investors through the Harvard Business School Club in Cleveland. I remember jeweler Larry Robinson, *"The Diamond Man,"* put money in, and he said, *"Mal, I will work on getting people into wheelchairs who don't even need them!"*

One of my investors was a man named Evan Kemp who was a dedicated activist in Washington. He had been a high school classmate of J.B. Richey and was a force behind the Americans with Disabilities Act. He even took on Jerry Lewis and the MDA Telethon about how that event demeaned people with disabilities, making donors feel pity so they would give money. But Kemp taught me a lot about disabilities and attitudes. For example, when you talk to a disabled person, you don't stand above them and look down. You kneel at their level. They don't like being called cripples or whatever. So I started to fight for them and join what they're trying to get done. And I think that attitude-wise, that helped me a lot in terms of being in tune with their needs.

Dan Moore III and Bill Jones were two other investors. Moore is from Cleveland; he is a very successful entrepreneur. I met him at the Harvard Business School Club of Northeastern Ohio. I asked him if there was any connection to the Dan T. Moore Hall, the officers' club in Fort Sill, Okla. He said it was named after his great-grandfather who rode with Teddy Roosevelt and the Rough Riders and founded the method of indirect fire of artillery. We became friends; he knew Barbara growing up, but I did not know him until I came to Cleveland. He joined my board of directors.

Bill Jones is older than I am, and he is another investor who is very entrepreneurial. The two of them helped me buy Invacare. By that I mean we would sit and plot how we could do this, how we could do that. Bill served as chairman of Invacare for a number of years.

Stan Pace, president of TRW, and later CEO of General Dynamics, was another investor. He liked the opportunity so much that he sent in an additional $50,000 to invest after we sewed up the deal. He said, *"If anybody drops out, I want in."* Well, a doctor who was interested sent my contract over to his lawyer — and the lawyer wanted to change something in the contract. I told him, *"My friend, it's too late. I'm not going to go changing anything."* So he withdrew his $50,000, and Stan Pace's extra $50,000 went in. Too bad for the doctor; he would have made multimillions out of it.

Other investors included J.B.'s brother DeWayne Richey, F.J. *"Joe"* Callahan, Whitney Evans, William A. Mitchell, Robert Files, Dr. Everett James, John W. Wilhelm, Dr. Ronald Ross and Robert G. Patterson. They bought $1.35 million of common and preferred stock.

I took a 15 percent interest in the common shares of the company for myself, so I had my $10,000 and $40,000 loans from friends and $100,000 borrowed from the company in a note.

My search for investors could have come to a tragic end on Oct. 3, 1979. I had a close call with a Connecticut tornado — and it could have blown away my chances to buy Invacare as it almost blew me away. I was looking for financing to make the transaction happen and was talking to Aetna in Hartford, Conn., about investment possibilities.

I came out of the Aetna office, and the sky was very dark. The clouds were moving fast, and it looked like there was going to be a tornado (remember, I was raised in Tornado Alley USA). I said so to my cab driver, and he responded, *"We don't have them in this part of the country."* So we started off for the airport, and it was raining and hailing like hell. All of a sudden, our cab spun around. The windows popped out, and we were in the middle of an F4 tornado. There were wires all over the street, poles down and everything. The cab driver had to back up an on-ramp to find our way to the airport.

Soon, he pulled up to a little liquor store that was still open and had a working phone. I waited in line (there were no cell phones in those days) and called Barbara. I said, *"I'm going to be late. I don't think I'm going to be in until tomorrow. I've been in a tornado."* So Barbara said in disbelief, *"Sure you have."* I said, *"Go turn on the TV and watch. It's the only tornado I think Hartford's ever had, and I'm in it. They closed the airport."* I couldn't fly out because the tornado had hit the airport, nearly hitting a plane trying to land. We couldn't even move the taxi. So we had a few beers there just waiting to move. Finally, the roads were opened and the cab driver found me a motel. I flew back to Cleveland the following morning — and never got any interest from Aetna.

Closing the deal

Believe it or not, I was third in line to buy Invacare. The fellow who was first in line was a wealthy Clevelander who wanted certain guarantees that Technicare Chairman Dick Grimm was unwilling to give. He wanted guarantees on receivables, and finally, Grimm said if the money was not in the bank on a certain day, this deal was off. Well, the deal fell through, but I still didn't get to be first in line. I had to get behind the second guy, the lawyer who worked for Technicare. He had the money, and he could have bought 100 percent of the company himself.

If I had the money then that I have now, I would have bought the whole company outright. Since that was not an option, our strategy was a leveraged buyout. Here's how a leveraged buyout works: First of all, check if they own real estate. You sell it to somebody and lease it back from them. That's what I did, which meant I now had to pay rent, but we received cash of $2 million. A bank will generally loan 50 percent on the inventory and 85 percent on receivables. After the sale leaseback and bank loan, there is an amount left unfunded in the purchase price generally higher than that amount, and that's called the *"plug"* figure. That's what you have to put in as equity in some form. In our case we put in $1 million of common and $500,000 of preferred stock in Invacare.

I really didn't have any money — but the attorney had never operated a company before. I hadn't either, but I had business experience, and he had been a lawyer all his life. Because of his relationship to Grimm, Grimm gave him second dibs on buying the company. In talking with the lawyer, we worked out an arrangement. Since he had no operating experience, he would be CEO, and I would be COO. So we were trying to get the financing together to do this thing, and I had to do all the work! He wasn't doing any of it; he was almost a reluctant buyer.

What I am about to tell you is really weird. We got the financing worked out, we were ready to go, and we were closing in a few days — and the lawyer called me into his office. *"Mal,"* he said, *"I've decided I am not going to do this." "Really?"* I said. *"Have you told your boss?" "No."* Then he said, *"I've got to go pick up my kids at school now. You tell him."* Now I didn't know Dick Grimm from anybody, but I asked to see him. I went to his office and Grimm said, *"Are you getting ready to close this deal?"* And I said, *"Yup, yes."* But I said, *"There's one thing you ought to know, Dick."* He said, *"All right, tell me." "Your attorney decided he's not going to buy it — but I want to buy it."* Grimm said, *"Are you kidding me?"*

Anyway, while I was talking to Grimm, the attorney came back in the office, as calm as can be. Grimm said, *"Mal has told me that you decided not to buy the company."* The lawyer said, *"Yeah, I decided not to buy the company."* So Grimm said to me. *"All right, you've got two weeks to close this thing."* That would be the end of the year. And I said incredulously, *"You gave him six months, and you give me two weeks?"* He said, *"If this isn't off our books by the end of the year, I am turning it over to J&J to let their department of acquisitions and mergers dispose of it."*

So anyway, I went home, thinking. We were buying Invacare for $1.5 million in equity, and I was both excited and nervous. I got a call from the lawyer's brother. *"I was talking to my brother and we would like to invest in your company,"* he said. *"He's decided not to run it."* I asked, *"How much would you like to invest?"* He set an amount that would have given him control of the company. I said, *"Well, that's controlling interest. Why don't you invest something less than that?"* No, he didn't want to do that. All of a sudden, it hit me. His brother had chastised the lawyer to the point that they had come to rebuy the company; I said no.

To find a bank to finance my bid to buy Invacare, I had to go out of state. I arranged for a $4.3 million loan from First Chicago Bank. The guy in first place had tied up the Cleveland banks. And it was hard enough for me as it was. I borrowed at 3 percent over the prime interest rate, and then during the real estate crash, prime went to 21 percent in the first 12 months. So we were paying 24 percent interest. At the very end of the negotiations, the bank said it wanted a $1 million life insurance policy on me. I said to myself, *"I'll never get a life insurance policy; I just had had cancer."* So I really got worried, but I was able to get a policy at only a slightly elevated premium — merely because I didn't smoke. And I was stunned. They weren't worried about the cancer, but they were worried about the smoking, which kind of made me feel like, well, maybe I won't die. I was able to get the policy. I never mentioned to the bank that I had cancer earlier.

For those parts of the deal to happen, I ran up a $50,000 bill with Calfee, Halter & Griswold for legal work with Dale LaPorte. I didn't know how I was going to pay that off. That was a lot of money in those days. So I offered Dale stock instead of cash. But he didn't take it. It would be worth several million dollars now had he accepted. I offered him the same deal later when we purchased Royal Appliance. It would've been worth several million dollars, but the firm just wanted cash. We joke about that still.

Next, we did a sale leaseback on the property but the potential buyers at the end wanted more money in escrow and wanted five of the 20 acres I had with Invacare. Finally, after more negotiations, Jeff and Pete Smythe agreed to the original deal that we had negotiated. We ran around and got the thing closed on the last working day of the year, which Grimm had set for the deadline. I remember those last few nights, I don't know if I got any sleep or not. It was like trying to hold a broken fence together with bailing wire. You shoved here and pushed there. Anyway, we got it done.

When I got to Invacare, keep in mind that I had just paid $1.5 million in equity for the company and the rest was the lease on the building and a bank loan. So you take $7.8 million — subtract $2 million for the building and property on Taylor Street in Elyria, Ohio, leaving $5.8 million, subtract $1.5 million of equity, which leaves $4.3 million to be covered by a bank loan.

Did I learn about risk from all this? You know, it wasn't that big of a risk. A lot of people think I took a big risk. I personally signed a $4.3 million loan. The biggest risk was that right at the end, the bank said I had to take a physical and get a life insurance policy. I didn't know if I could get a policy with my cancer history. That was the gamble right there — that after all my work, it might be a health issue that threw a monkey wrench in the deal.

When we officially took control of Invacare on Dec. 28, 1979, Invacare was not well-respected in the health care products industry. Annual sales were flat at about $19 million. Our chief competitor, Everest & Jennings, had sales of $125 million, a profit after tax of $7 million and book net worth of $75 million. We had substantial debt, no new products were under development, product quality and delivery were poor, Elyria was a high-labor cost area, Taiwan was emerging as cheaper off-shore competition, there was no international business of any consequence, the company had no strategy or business plan, and the new CEO, that's me, had never run a company before!

I've been told that some years ago they taught my case at a local bank to young bankers, and they describe Invacare in the conditions under which I bought it. Most of the young bankers in the classes said they wouldn't do it.

I had no idea what we could do at Invacare. I thought I could just run the company, and we'd probably have a little niche. If you were to tell me we would have $1.8 billion in sales 32 years later, I would've said you were crazy.

At first, no respect

During my first sales calls in 1980, most customers were quick to tell me all the things wrong with Invacare and our products. I call that the Rodney Dangerfield era — I got no respect. But I looked at it this way: You pick any company in Cleveland, go out and interview people about the company, and you will find something that needs to change. It may be that the product is not so bad. Maybe they just want it lighter, they want it for less money or want it faster. But you'll find that they want something.

I would basically hear how screwed up Invacare was, and I said, *"Well, gee, if it had been such a great company, I couldn't have bought it for $8 million."* So we went about the fundamentals of business trying to build better products, design better products, hire a better sales organization and give better service. Our strategy hasn't changed substantially from the principles that we think are important to building a good business. You can fool customers once, but generally not the second time around. The importance of quality, performance, having good price points, deliveries, having a great sales organization to represent the company — are all key points.

I continue to learn from large and small companies, and usually the innovators are the ones that really bring change. Invacare has been very innovative in a number of ways. I try to keep our company entrepreneurial and to talk about guiding principles, directions and strategy, but I let my people take the ball and run with it and have the freedom and speed they need to make changes to adapt to their environment.

We've seen tremendous change over the 32 years I've been in the business. I remember the day the Taiwanese entered into the business. I remember names that were almost like Hallmark cards in our industry: Everest & Jennings, Smith and Davis, Lumex, Mountain Medical. Some of those names are not competitors anymore. Then we had Sunrise and Graham-Field as the industry began to consolidate. We have new competitors like every 10 years. Someone new emerges, and we have to change how we do things, but there are certain things we don't change and those are the guiding principles.

I still think of Invacare as a small company in a lot of ways because we're still flexible and we can move and make changes, and we don't have to deal with large committees and bureaucratic decision-making. The nice thing about a small company, you can be light on your feet and move and do things and be innovative, and that's what large companies have to guard against as they get larger. They must avoid getting bogged down.

I honestly didn't know anything about wheelchairs, but I went out and found out that Everest & Jennings, our major competitor, was held in ill repute by its customers. The company was arrogant and treated people with disabilities like they were cripples. The wheelchairs looked ugly and heavy. Everest & Jennings had no sensitivity to their customers — I mean none.

So I started studying Invacare's product line. Some products were obsolete; with some others, we were losing money. I told our engineers to develop some innovative products. We would offer what Everest & Jennings was failing to offer. They may have had more than an 80 percent share of the U.S. wheelchair market, but they were losing touch with their customers.

Right after we bought Invacare, I got a call from the vice president of sales of a company called Smith & Davis. At that time, the company had about 70 percent of the U.S. bed market. The VP said to me that he wanted to buy Invacare. *"Well, I just bought the company two weeks ago,"* I said. *"I don't think we'd sell it."* He said, *"But if you don't sell it to me, we're going to go into the wheelchair business."* I said, *"Well, I will meet with you."* So I met with him at the Sheraton Airport Hotel, and he proceeded to describe to me how the bed fits like a glove with the wheelchair, bought from the same dealers, the same customers, same, same, same. He convinced me. So I left that meeting, but told him no. He went into the wheelchair business; I went into the bed business — and I took it over. I eventually tried to buy him (it was blocked by the FTC) and subsequently took bed share leadership in the market. So today, we have the leading share of the home-care bed business.

But this little story was an odd one because I wasn't even in the bed business. It shows the advantage of what I said about being flexible and nimble. I probably eventually would have entered the bed market on my own, but I would have had to learn where it fit. The Smith & Davis VP did all my homework for me.

There were some little companies that were competitors, but really, we only had one major competitor at that time, Everest & Jennings. It was about $120 million, and we were $19 million. E&J was about six or seven times our size. It was a public company and was moving into a brand-new facility in Camarillo, Calif. At that point, E&J got all screwed up with its computers and customer orders were lost, and that helped us. Customers were looking for something better. We stepped up to the plate.

Basically, all we made were standard, manual Medicare-type wheelchairs, not the upper-end, lightweight ones, and we made some patient aids such as commodes and walkers. As I began to learn more about the business, I learned there were lots of products that could be sold by the same sales force through the same home medical equipment providers. The average Invacare salesperson at that time sold about $1 million a year. There were 19 salespeople, so we had about $19 million in sales. Over a three-year period, I replaced 17 out of 19 salespeople because they were just order takers; they weren't salespeople. I replaced most of them, and I think our salespeople today do $6 million to $7 million each in annual sales.

When I was looking for new salespeople, I interviewed candidates; it was a big part of what I did. It was important to me so I took the time to make judgments on the people. Since we didn't have any new products in development, we really had to rely on the strengths of our sales force. With their effort, in my first year running Invacare, it went from $19 million to $25 million in sales. I think I only had one new product that year.

I was a big believer in sales. I was a young guy; I knew that I could affect the sales. I mean I could get a million-dollar customer, and that just made the company grow 5 percent. I felt like I could personally move the needle at that time. And the more I got salespeople who were good, then the more we would all move the needle.

To a large extent, I wanted to be out there selling my products. I always had been an external person. I like the external part of Invacare more than the internal part. Some people love to be in the factory or in the office … but I love to be out with customers. Not only could I sell, I could learn what I needed to go back and change about Invacare or find if there was a problem or an opportunity. I wasn't a theorist. I mean I really lived the life of a salesman. I knew all the salespeople by their first names; I knew who they were. We would have sales meetings and that sort of thing. I kept my tabs on the high performers.

About two weeks after I had been on the job, the vice president of sales, an ex-Johnson & Johnson guy who smoked like a fiend, and my guess was he probably had been canned from J&J — he wouldn't otherwise be in a little company like Invacare — came into my office and said he was owed a bonus. Well, I had bought the company from J&J, but I didn't know about any bonus, so I said, *"Look, this is a new entity. Your beef is with the previous owners, you know?"* I just thought it was a screw-up. So he left. And he came back a couple of days later, and said if I didn't pay him the bonus, he was going to resign. I'm not big on threats, anyway, so I said, *"When are you resigning?"* He replied it would be in a year. I said, *"That's really nice of you to give me that much warning before you resign."* If it had been a threat in any other area, I probably would've been nervous, but he was in sales and that's my area. I wasn't impressed with this guy. So I said, *"Well, I don't think I'm going to need you that long."* He said, *"How long are you going to need me?"* I said, *"Uh, take a half-hour or an hour. I don't care. Just clean out your desk."* He had talked himself out of a job.

Pat Nalley joins the fold

One of the things I wanted to do once I got to Invacare was to look up Pat Nalley, who had been the vice president of sales at Harris-Seybold when I was there. He's deceased now, but he certainly played a big role in shaping Invacare. Pat had retired to Baton Rouge and gone into the real-estate business. He retired at 65, but he was a young 65 and very dynamic. So I called him when I got to Invacare, and I said, *"Pat, I would like you to come up, look the company over and see what you think of it — and see if you think you would like to join us."* He asked, *"What are you selling?"* *"Wheelchairs,"* I said. He said, *"How much do they sell for?"* *"A couple hundred bucks,"* I said. Keep in mind that he had never sold anything for less than $15,000 and up to $1 million. Pat said, *"Mal, how the hell do you make any money, selling something for 200 bucks?"* I laughed, *"Pat, we are going to sell a lot of them!"*

Anyway, I got him to come to Invacare, and he helped me build a great sales force. To this day we have the E. Patrick *"Pat"* Nalley Award for an outstanding salesperson who for three years in a row has achieved great results — somebody who was tried and true, not a one-year flash in the pan. Pat taught me really how to sell and I learned that no matter what the situation was, there was a positive spin on the thing. He was a master at it. I remember when I worked for him that we had a big account that was having problems with its press. Our service manager said his people were all tied up, and he couldn't get a serviceman there until Friday. The account was not happy. They called Pat and he said, *"Now, I want to make it very clear. I'm going to make you the No. 1 priority ... blah, blah, blah... I'm taking these guys, getting them off their jobs, and we will be there by Friday."* Well, that was the same day that the service manager said before! But Pat explained it in a way that the customer liked — he made them feel that they were important, that they were the priority.

One day at a show in Atlanta where we had a booth, a lot of people were there, and this one guy complained that he couldn't get close enough to see the product. He wanted to have a demonstration. He was complaining and Pat said, *"Did you ever stop and think why you can't get closer to the product?"* The guy said no. *"The reason you can't is because it is so good, the product is so outstanding, that the people are just coming here in droves to see it. And if you just wait a little bit, I will get you a demo."* Pat had a knack for turning things around. He could take the darkest picture and turn it into light. So I learned that from him besides learning specifics on how to handle a situation. We had a lot of fun together He helped me sort out the good guys.

Even though Pat worked under me at Invacare and I had reported to him at Harris, it worked out very well. We became really close friends. We respected each other. As I told you, he was a very good judge of salesmanship. Together, we built a formidable sales organization.

I remember sitting in an Invacare meeting early on, and I asked something and someone on the staff said, *"You can't do that."* I said, *"You know, I hate that word, can't. I don't want you ever to use it again. You might tell me how much money it will take or how long it will take, but don't use can't."* We became a *"can-do"* organization. In the early days, I kept talking about how we were going to be No. 1 in wheelchairs. I think people thought I was a smart-aleck MBA who would probably last about six months. But at some point, I can't tell you when, the engineers and the people actually started believing that we could do it. We started gaining on E&J, they kept screwing up, and we kept gaining customers and knocking them off. Pretty soon, you could feel the energy in the company that we were going to be No. 1.

So this attitude eventually became winning — and it took a while. I can remember when the engineers used to leave right on time, but pretty soon they started staying and working late because they felt they could win. We faced a giant monopolist, E&J, but that attitude still pervades the company today. People want to win. And if you have a product that's a superior product, you want to win with that product. Those days were a lot of fun.

Now, about 1980-81 after I bought Invacare, E&J launched a special program almost simultaneously with the introduction of Invacare's first power wheelchair. I was leaving on vacation and they announced an 18 percent discount on standard wheelchairs — with free freight. So it was a total of 23 percent. All I made was basic standard wheelchairs and other patient aids. So Pat Nalley called me about it and met me at the airport. We had to decide pretty damn fast what we were going to do. I said either we were in the business, or we were not in the business. We met them head-on. They were trying to put us under. The Invacare people reacted very positively — somehow our sales went way the hell up. E&J, being a public company, could not take it too long. They couldn't keep it permanently. The incident actually turned out to be a real test for our company. We got through it, and finally, E&J backed off.

Initially, I figured there were several ways that Invacare could increase profits. The easiest was to increase prices. The second was to sell more products. The third was to cut expenses, and the fourth was to lower manufacturing costs. I decided I would just take a chance and raised prices 5 percent. It stuck. So you figure 5 percent of $19 million, that's a million bucks. So we made $1.4 million that first year due to the price increase and a $6 million increase in sales. We improved receivables by 30 days, too. We increased the inventory turns. We did all of it, and we never looked back.

I had a lawyer look through all our patents just for the heck of it. I found out that E&J was infringing on an old patent we had for what we called a Swing Away. You tap a bar on a wheelchair and the footrests swing away. So we sued them over it. They kept trying to negotiate with us, and I said I would settle for $1 million. They offered a half-million, then $600,000. Then they offered me $950,000. Finally, we both agreed to a $1 million settlement. I still have a copy of the check. So I look back at that and can say that they really subsidized the $1.5 million in purchase price.

J.B., innovations and acquisitions

In 1984, I brought J.B. Richey on full-time at Invacare; he had been on the board of directors since 1980. J.B. told me he always wanted to be an engineer. As a little kid, he would run around with extension cords plugging in everything. When he got to be a teenager, he used to fix TVs, which were new at that time. He just loved electronics.

On the other hand, I'm a person who can't fix a light switch. I'm not very technical, but I know what customers want. J.B. and I actually hit it off as friends. We both were interested in developing new products.

J.B. and I have had great success at being able to tell if products are really good or not at all. We've looked at many ideas. There are two parts to it. Is it a good technology, and secondly, is the product idea good? That's key in creating products and then companies.

We could think on our on our feet and be innovative.

J.B. thinks like I do in that he believes he can't be afraid to try new things and new technologies that come out. You know, they just might hit and then you're going to have a wildly successful product. If you fail, try something else. Don't give up, but just keep doing it.

I relied on him to lead the effort to start designing a motorized wheelchair. So together, we developed a chair. Then almost to the day that I introduced our motorized chair, E&J discounted its standard wheelchair, I guess trying to scare me out of business.

I look back to when I first walked around the company. I asked what are we, what business are we in? The associates said we are a standard manual wheelchair company — everyone would say it. We didn't do business anywhere except in the United States, not even in Canada. We went from a U.S. standard wheelchair company to a home health care equipment company, to an international home health care manufacturer. Today, we are trying to become a more clinically oriented company; in other words, expanding into wound care, oxygen, treating decubitus ulcers and other therapy. So I think we will be known as a worldwide clinically oriented and long-term care company because now we do long-term care, not just home care. We are pursuing that patient who is at home or in a facility who is still a long-term care patient. Today, we are in 80 countries; when I started, we were in one. The stories about how we got there and everything are interesting, and you wake up one day and there you are. I think we've done 60 acquisitions. It sounds like a lot, but when you figure it's been 32 years, it's been about two a year.

One form of acquisition gives us a product that we know could be sold through the same channel. Another form of acquisition gives us a geographical presence, such as buying a French company gives you France. We bought the No. 1 company in France. I'm not telling you that I am a dealmaker in that sense, but generally, it has to be a win-win for both sides. When a guy wants to cash in and we need him, if it fits, we will deal. Generally, I didn't try to cram an acquisition down the throat of my people. I try to get them thirsty for it.

When I did buy a certain company, I can tell you the reason for every one of them. Most of them added products to our line. For instance, I bought a bed company in Florida that never shipped a bed — but they had a design. I didn't have any money so I sold them on the idea of royalties. They looked at Invacare and felt our company could sell the bed. I said, *"If we are successful, I will pay royalties."* So I paid them $3 million in royalties from sales.

Once I bought a little oxygen concentrator company up in Connecticut. There were 40 other similar companies at the time, and this one wasn't any different from any of the others, but we worked it and made it the No. 1 company.

I once said that there were no magic tricks at Invacare, just sound execution of basics. We just sold better than other people sold, we manufactured better quality, we engineered better. What I mean was it wasn't one thing, some great idea. We just had good engineering and selling, good manufacturing, we expanded a line, we expanded the geographical reach and just kept executing. It was each part of our team doing what it did best. We would buy a company, use our huge selling organization — and all of a sudden, you've got 100 people selling the product. We used our distribution strength a lot of times when we would buy a small company.

Success breeds success. If you do a few things and you pull it off well, people start to say, *"Maybe this guy knows what he is talking about."* They're willing to try a new thing. I think the fact that we are union-free, that we are innovative and willing to try new things, and that we are always pursuing excellence proves to everybody that I wanted to be the best. I competed when I worked for Ohio-Nuclear; I was competing against giants such as General Electric, Picker and Siemens. All of a sudden, I was competing against E&J. They were not good managers. Competitors I was used to going up against were better players, but E&J was still a pretty significant challenge. You have to choose your battles. I mean it was certainly an unsettling thing, and I didn't look forward to having to cut my price to compete with E&J, but I remember we kept growing — and at one point, we ran out of money.

It was a moment of truth. I had to go public. I looked into private equity and the investors wanted twice the amount of Invacare than the public offering was to propose. If a venture capitalist would buy 20 percent of Invacare, the public market would take 10 percent of the company for the same dollars. So we had two public offerings. And then when we got into financial trouble later; that was scary. I had to go back out and do some repackaging.

During that time, I got a little too aggressive, and I got too much debt and violated a bank covenant. But you know, you drive to work every day and your mind is going a mile a minute and you're trying to be better every day, and after a lot of years, it was more important to me to be successful in business than anything else. If it hadn't been for Barbara raising our two kids — not that I wasn't around, but my mind was on the business — we would have been up the creek.

Dealing with the pains of growth

I will never forget when Invacare started a little company in Ireland. We had the idea of shipping parts to Ireland and assembling them there to sell in Europe. Well, that didn't work out. It cost more to ship the parts, and by the time you got the parts all cleaned up and assembled, it cost more than shipping the whole wheelchair.

Our manager, Pat and I had gone out to dinner, and the manager said on the way home, *"Do you mind if we all hold hands and pray for the company?"* I said, *"What?!"* He thought the company was going to go under, and we had to pray. I said, *"Oh, Pat [Nalley], we're in trouble!"* Little did we know trouble would come. ... We ended up shutting down the joint venture.

But by trying to do business in Europe, we stumbled upon the companies that we eventually bought. I bought a wheelchair company in England and another tiny company in Germany. The guy who ran the company in Germany, its sales were $1 or $2 million, had been the chief engineer of the No. 1 wheelchair company in Germany. After a falling out with the president of that company, he started his own company. He didn't have much money, but he sure knew how to design a chair. I bought him out.

We then made several acquisitions. Eventually, a major opportunity came along, Poirier in France. Poirier was the leading maker of wheelchairs in that country and the leading maker of lightweight wheelchairs in Europe. Then we had a major acquisition in Sweden, Beram AB, a distributor of wheelchairs and other rehabilitative products. We put it all together to where we were the No. 1 home care manufacturing company in Europe.

We bought 60 companies and 60 brand names, and we had to change them quietly. We added Invacare to their names. In some cases, we took their brand name, made it the product name and added ours as the brand name. For example, you will still see the Invacare logo on the Top End chair and the sports wheelchairs made in Tampa. We kept Top End as the product name and added our logo on the chair. Now it's Top End by Invacare. We are trying to build our brand in new markets by leveraging the familiar names people knew.

Speaking of sports wheelchairs, about the late 1980s and early 1990s, wheelchair sports took off. It's also when Invacare launched a line of lightweight sports wheelchairs called the Action line. They were made of materials such as aluminum and titanium — tough and lightweight stuff. We sponsor a group of elite wheelchair athletes, Team Invacare, and they serve as ambassadors around the world for Invacare. They compete in the Paralympics Games and other events.

We had acquired Top End in 1993, and it became the sports wheelchair division of Invacare. I felt that meeting the needs of sports wheelchair users was a vital need to fill for us to be successful in this niche.

While I was working on acquisitions, we also worked on innovations of all types. I think we had the first financing program, called Invalease. We had the concept of one-stop shopping before anyone else did. No one's been able to quite copy us. We can deliver a whole gamut of products from one warehouse. Most companies we competed with were one-product companies. In terms of innovations, we had the first microprocessor-controlled wheelchair. You could program the chair with its computer. We had the first split screen, one-man delivery bed. We've always been innovative. I can't say the products have been the scale of Apple computer or something like that, but they've always been out front and ahead of what the competition was doing.

Most people try to copy us, and you know if you try to copy someone, that person never sits still. So if you copy them, they move. We kept being innovative and continued to think about how to be better. You don't just freeze. Something you hear frequently is, *"If it ain't broke, don't fix it."* I don't believe in that. I believe everything can be improved. We look for continuous improvement in everything we do.

What I'm saying is that if you think something you make is good, there is somebody out there trying to design it better than what you're doing. It used to be about four to five weeks for the delivery on a wheelchair. Now it's four or five days — and we are trying to figure out how to do it faster than that. While that's very good, it doesn't mean it can't be better. If you collect your accounts receivables in three days, it doesn't mean you can't collect in two or one. Your attitude always should be — how do I make this better? So we've never arrived. We've never said that we've arrived.

Leading by example and earning respect

I had the opportunity to teach my people at Invacare the leadership principles I learned in the Marines and from my experiences. Here they are:

- **Set yourself as an example.** Don't ask your people to do more than you do. The Marine Corps teaches you never to ask your people to do more than you are willing to do yourself. That simply means you set the example. In business, if you are unwilling to take the red-eyes to California or to confront the tough problems, how can you expect your people to want to do that?

- **Develop loyalty downward.** Care about your people first. Some people have trouble with that one, but what it really means is do I care more about Mal Mixon, or do I care more about my team? I always feel that I want my people to be well-paid. I want them to have stock options. I want them to be able to become wealthy. And if they are, I am automatically wealthy and successful. The same is true in any team-working effort, whether it's in the military or not. You're only as good as your team.

- **Develop an interest in your teammates and their families — as people.** Your team is made up of individuals; they are not really made of the same material. They have personal goals and problems. They have health problems. They have personal ambitions and motivations. They have a lot of things. And you've got to understand them and individually deal with the issues.

- **Make integrity a priority.** Never make a promise that you do not intend to honor or keep. That is simply a matter of ethics. We've built plants in Mexico and China, and I went in to our American factories and told them I was going to do it, and I told them why I was going to do it. I didn't lie to them. I told them how it would affect employment. My people can trust me. They know that I tell them the truth. I never lie to them. I think that sometimes we agree to something and maybe it doesn't work out quite the way we had hoped, but I think it is important to follow through. If you tell someone you are going to do something, don't be a wimp, don't cry at the first sight of blood and don't walk away from a tough situation. Sometimes, it is the stick-to-itiveness that causes it to happen. We all know about some tough business situations where people thought their companies were going to go south but they hung in there, a miracle happened and they held on.

- **Keep your tenacity and resolution strong.** Cultivate an unfaltering determination to achieve your plans and goals. You make a plan and things are never going to happen exactly the way you think they are going to happen. I have had some of the most talented failures come to me with beautiful charts and explain to me how they failed. And I have also had people who didn't go to Harvard or any college at all, who weren't very articulate, were nervous in front of a crowd and who got great results. Some people just get discouraged easily when something doesn't quite go right; they think, *"Well, I can't do that; the competition did this."* You really have to have a killer mentality about getting it done. I think we have a team of people at Invacare that do that sort of thing.

- **Become a professional expert.** A snow job never works. Develop an expertise in your field. A person comes into our company — if they are a phony, they are going to be known within 30 days. You can't fool people very long. I've always advised people: become an expert at something. Become a great marketer, a great engineer, a great operating person or whatever. Become an expert in your field.

- **Emphasize courage and honor.** Face difficult problems and circumstances squarely and lead where others may be apprehensive or unsure. You know, leaders have to tackle the tough problems and not the easy ones — those you get off your desk right away. You have to have the mentality of, *"I like to deal with problems. I like to fix things, because I know when I fix it, the company is going to be a lot better."*

Top management's most important function is leadership. I first wrote these leadership points in 1983, and I don't think my views about leadership have changed at all since then. You look back at the tests that we've had, the E&J test, the financial test, trials of running out of money, changing computers systems, which almost brought us to our knees. We've always gotten through them; they made us bigger, better, stronger.

The glass is half-full for me

In business, I think a lot of people don't know much about leadership, how to relate to people and how to manage people. Most people want to be on a team — and they want to be on a winning team. They don't want to be on a losing team. I never liked to have pessimists around me. I like people who want to get things done and think positively.

Many leaders want advice on how to deal with malcontents. If you've acquired a company and you have a negative-thinking executive on your hands, it's very, very difficult to get someone to change. As hard as you try — a lot of the time, managers spend weeks and months trying to correct somebody when they should be spending their time with the ones that are the winners because you get more results out of them. But we all seem to do it. We often try to give a person another chance or two.

I asked a famous doctor at the Cleveland Clinic once what he did when he had a doctor who didn't quite measure up to the Clinic's standards. *"Do you fire him, like I do at Invacare?"* I asked.

He said, *"Oh no, we don't fire him."*

"What do you do?" I asked.

"I put my hand on his shoulder and I say, *'Son, you're going to enjoy practicing in Kansas.' We just farm them out there."*

Well, that's kind of what they call the Greyhound Therapy — send them off on a long bus ride and he becomes somebody else's problem at the other end. But you try to work with people as best you can. I think we all probably waste time trying to get them to change. I always try to go the extra mile with a person. I never fired anyone for making a mistake — maybe for incompetence but not a mistake.

A lot of people are afraid they are going to make a mistake. I don't want my people to believe that I don't want them to think aggressively. If you act aggressively, you're going to make mistakes sometimes, but in that way, you are on the leading edge of things. If you are right or wrong, you're still going to do pretty damn good. But if you keep making the same mistake over and over again, that ain't too smart. I've had to replace some people, but by and large, I find that most people properly motivated, properly paid and properly in the right slot, can do pretty damn good. When I took over Invacare, I didn't let many people go. But by and large, I worked with the people who were there. I had to put some in certain slots, that sort of thing, but I didn't fire them all. I did, however, have to clean house in the sales department of all but two because it was a totally different mentality there. But I am not the kind of guy who goes around firing a bunch of people. I try to work with them and give them a chance. Now if you do all those things and it doesn't work, that's a different thing. It's time to move on.

Testing the Mixon mettle

By 1984, Invacare sales were rising at a 38 percent annual rate, but that meant debt was accumulating, too. We were borrowing to support our growth. We decided that a public offering was the best way for us to raise the necessary funds to continue our growth.

But it turns out, we were a year late. If we had gone public a year earlier, we'd have found a very bullish market with people paying high prices for new issues. I was hoping for $14 to $16 a share, and we only got $11. So the IPO raised less than what we wished for (we have since split the stock twice).

The main thing is — we made it through these challenges. There were quality problems that year with the oxygen concentrator, and on top of that, the federal government changed the reimbursement policy for wheelchairs. It was like the Man Upstairs had it in for us that year. The other thing was that we were now public, which meant I had to deal with things in a public manner. The public exposure and disclosure practices take you away from the freedom of running a private business — decisions are scrutinized by shareholders, media and others.

It takes quite a bit of time to prepare news releases, to answer questions from investors and media, and to meet with investors. First, there's a time factor for the chief executive who might better spend that time running the business. However, that's a necessity if you're going to be fair to your investors. Second, I think the whole disclosure area is frustrating because it transmits to our competitors a whole lot of things about our strengths and weaknesses. Third, there are a lot of additional costs involved in going public. You have to make annual 10-K reports, quarterly 10-Qs and reports to the SEC on everything from profit-sharing plans to stock options. Our lawyers do those filings and they run up a pretty big bill. But all in all, I think the pluses of being a public company outweigh the minuses.

We took cost-cutting measures, introduced new products, and by 1986, we were moving Invacare forward. We introduced a lot of products in 1990, more than 50. I didn't forget about acquisitions, either. One thing that gave us more visibility was our purchase of Top End Wheelchair Sports. Athletes use Top End's products in wheelchair sporting events, including NBA-sponsored basketball games. We made them lighter and faster than the competition.

By the end of the 1990s, Invacare had racked up 35 acquisitions. But the Chinese and their low-cost production gave us a run for our money. We were making record profits in 2004, our European divisions were expanding — and we decided to fight the Chinese manufacturers in their own battle by taking some globalization efforts, such as sourcing materials and components and making products at two Chinese plants.

What this shows is when you have a problem, you have to work your way through it. Invacare's got a hell of a challenge right now with national *"suicide bidding"* (coercing providers to bid at unsustainable Medicare reimbursement rates) for reimbursement of home medical equipment and FDA regulations. And we'll get through it, I have no doubts.

You can use a lot of different means to get through challenges. Gerry Blouch, now Invacare's CEO, likes to tell the story how I was, in effect, the ultimate diplomat at what was a *"near-international incident."* Once, Gerry and I were visiting a company in Germany that we had been courting for some time. The CEO, who was the son of the founder, took us out to one of the finest, most renowned restaurants in town. The proprietor of the restaurant, who was a friend of our host, invited us to see the wine cellar. He claimed to have the best wines of the region and offered us a taste.

With a touch of arrogance, he displayed his five best bottles of wine. This guy then worked his way through each of them with a detailed background and commentary on the quality of every swirl, smell and sip. Finally, the proprietor finished his little dissertation with a loud and firm disclosure that this wine came from a region that had been heavily bombed by the Americans in World War II. The mood darkened. My German host shifted uncomfortably on his feet. He was obviously embarrassed. So I broke the painful silence with a big grin: *"Now that you mention it, it does have a faint metallic taste."* Everybody who was tense became calm, and we all had a laugh. What had been an awkward moment got smoothed out. I guess I won the statesman award for that night.

I think I have a natural ability to *"ad lib"* — say or do something unrehearsed, on the spot. I was always on my toes during sales calls and pretty much all the time. I was in Tampa a few years back visiting a big Invacare customer; it was a courtesy call. We had dinner and played golf. There were four of us guys: Mike Parsons and Lou Slangen from Invacare, myself and the sales manager from the California infusion pump company we had acquired. We were staying at a plush hotel, and it had a winding road to its entrance bordered with trees and bushes. We got out of our cab and started walking down the road. All of a sudden this car came up the road and stopped. Two guys were in it. One got out of the car and pointed a gun right at the guy next to me. I could see very clearly the barrel of the gun. He said, *"Give me your wallets or I will kill you."* So we all took off running in every direction!

People have argued with me over whether it would have been safer to hand over the wallets, but I instinctively ran. I remember I cut a zigzag course as if I were in combat and went through a hedge to get away. The gunman kind of trained his gun around on us, but he never did shoot anybody. We all eventually got to the hotel lobby, did high-fives and celebrated. But a minute later, the reality sunk it; we all said, *"Holy s---!"* after we realized what a close call we had.

The challenge of Washington

Invacare has had problems with Medicare reimbursement ever since I can remember. In the early years, it wasn't so bad, but the government changed the method of reimbursement in the 1980s. It really slowed down our growth. When Congress was debating the Americans with Disabilities Act, I decided it was time to look into the process. If the ADA passed (ADA became law in July 1990), it would reverberate throughout the health care industry. Public places had to be accessible to those in wheelchairs, which sounds fine because Invacare stands for more rights for the disabled, but

Medicare stuck to its restrictive reimbursement regulations, which didn't sound so good for Invacare.

I wanted the government to cap home medical equipment rental costs and allow Medicare recipients to get better equipment rather than just receive the bare bones essentials.

Two of my biggest customers called me one day and said they would like me to tackle Washington on this reimbursement issue. I realized nobody was representing my industry in Washington. So I started to get active, holding fundraisers and so on. I got involved deeper and deeper. I became close to some politicians — both Democrats and Republicans. I just wanted them to see the issues as I saw them.

It's an educational process. Politicians wanted to do the right things politically. Well, one day I woke up and found I had become the industry leader in that respect. Nobody else was doing what I was, I mean not even close.

In the early years at Invacare, I didn't care so much about reimbursement. I was focused on how to grow the business and on beating my competitors. Once I overcame my competitors, I realized that reimbursement was holding us back. A rising tide lifts all boats, you know. So I've tried to work on things that would elevate and help the industry — which would also benefit Invacare. It operates like this: The work that I do involving Washington is predicated on making sure our customers get reimbursement and are able to continue to buy our products and that helps the overall industry.

But the whole Washington scene reminds me of the Tar-baby, one of the old Uncle Remus stories by Joel Chandler Harris. In this story, Br'er Fox is trying to catch his nemesis, Br'er Rabbit.

Br'er Fox makes a small figure out of tar with buttons for eyes. He sets the Tar-baby along the path he knows Br'er Rabbit will walk along. When Br'er Rabbit sees the Tar-baby, he is naturally curious and says *"Howdy!"* to strike up a conversation. He gets frustrated when the Tar-baby won't talk to him. So Rabbit punches the Tar-baby and gets stuck in the tar. He struggles to get loose but the more he fights, the more stuck he gets. He's hopelessly trapped; he can't get out.

Working in Washington is like fighting the Tar-baby. You get in it, and then you can't get out. And it's like pushing a wet noodle uphill.

Everything else in my life I've been able to do with success. Being a perfectionist and after some time trying to work with Washington folks, I realized I've finally taken on something that I'd never get perfect. I think there's no vision of what our country wants with health care. We're like a Whac-a-Mole game — just hitting at random issues. But I have a clear vision, and I'm hoping a presidential candidate will come along that also has a vision.

Home health care can play a huge role in our health care system. But home care is only 2 percent of Medicare, and it's still embryonic. But that is my vision — home care should be more of an option. It's about one-sixth the cost of an institution. People want to be at home, and the infection rate is much lower at home. I feel home care is more cost-effective, it's preferred by patients, and it's safer in terms of reduced infection rates.

I've actually been able to achieve a few things for the industry. I was able to get the patient choice bill passed that allows you to pay for better equipment along with the Medicare reimbursement. Sen. George Voinovich, who was (he is retired now) a real fighter for our industry, helped with extending the reimbursement time for oxygen. I convinced the late U.S. Rep. Stephanie Tubbs Jones not to put rehab into competitive bidding regulations. These were some of the things that I've been able to achieve for the industry as a whole, not just for Invacare.

And, as they say, the beat goes on. ...

Chapter 8: Hooked on Deals

I admit it. I have an insatiable desire to do deals. I don't know why, but I know it gets my adrenaline going. It's been a hobby for me — some people collect stamps, I invest in entrepreneurial situations. I feel it's a lot less risky than, say, a dice game. So if I can try to affect that situation by exerting control and changing it, then it minimizes the risk. I'm not sure how I would characterize this, but I've done 60 deals that involved Invacare, and I've counted 45 independent deals. My wife, Barbara, says I am addicted to opportunity — even at the age of 72!

I often use a baseball metaphor about the success of a deal: a home run in terms of a deal is something that makes me a million or more dollars. Making a hundred thousand doesn't quite meet that measurement. Well, I don't call it a home run anymore. It's more like a single — ha ha.

I'll tell you a funny story. I was golfing with my friend and Invacare board member Ohio Gov. John Kasich at The Country Club in Pepper Pike one morning and Kasich was late. I was putting on the practice green while I waited. When he arrived, he came over to me, huffing and puffing. He said, *"Mal, you won't believe this. I got 30,000 bucks for one speech last night."* I said, *"You know, John, that's great. I've been sitting here putting, and I think Invacare's stock went up $2 million while I've been waiting for you."* He has never forgotten that story.

The point is, it's creation of capital. A lot of people do not understand capital formation. They understand wages, they're working for it. Athletes, movie stars and some newscasters make big bucks. But most people can't and won't ever make big bucks through wages. They've got to make it through capital creation. I feel until you own something, it is difficult to create capital. You know, you're starting out and maybe you're getting a reputation. Maybe someday you'll invent something and start your own company. Yes, I'm telling you to own a piece of the rock, and all your labor pays off for you because you're creating value.

Deal-making, step 1

To put a deal together, there are some principles that have guided me over my career. First, you have to give the principals an opportunity to gain wealth. You can do that by giving them part ownership. There are ways to ensure that they would make a lot of money if the deal is successful. Generally, I like to work with an entrepreneur who has his own money in the deal. If he doesn't, that makes me very nervous. It doesn't matter how much money. For example, there is an investor who is the president of a Florida enterprise I helped set up. He's running the operation. He doesn't have much money, but he put in a lot of what he had. So if you told me that you had $10,000 — that's all you had — and you put it all into the deal, that would impress me. If you told me you had $1 million and put in just $10,000, that wouldn't impress me.

The point I'm making is this, if an entrepreneur doesn't have his money in the deal, I'm not interested. One night I had a guy come to my house, and he was creating something called MBA magazine. He was a Harvard Business School and Law School graduate. I think he was a perpetual student, but he came from a wealthy family, and he had never really succeeded at anything. But he came to my house to get an investment from me, and I asked, *"How much do you have in the deal?"* It was some paltry sum … $10,000 or $20,000. I didn't even listen to the rest of his pitch because I knew his family members were multimillionaires. Anyway, he got every area CEO, every big name, to be in it, too. Well, I was sitting around the country club with my buddies, and they were telling me, *"You should've gotten into this, Mal. These are big-name guys."* And I was sitting there on the sidelines feeling like, *"Oh, gee, what a dummy I am."*

The premier issue of the magazine came out. First of all, I never thought there was a market; I don't read something because I'm an MBA. I read it because I'm a Sigma Alpha Epsilon, a Marine or stuff like that. Besides, I can't even define what an MBA is. Anyway, this first edition came out, and it was flawless. I mean it had color, great articles and a lot of unbelievable advertising. It was thick! I said to myself, *"Holy crap!"* Then I found out that, for the first edition, he gave free advertising — and the second edition never came out! One edition, no revenue, just lots of cost.

I always put money in a deal before I talk to somebody else about investing too, because I figure if they don't think I would invest in it, why should they invest? How can I tell you why you should invest in this when you can say, *"Well, Mal, how much do you have in it?"* And if I said, *"Nothing,"* that would make them very nervous; it would make me hesitant if I were in that position. It doesn't matter what the business is. I've been in all kinds of businesses and businesses I knew nothing about when I started, such as wheelchairs, vacuum cleaners, banking, soft-drink machines and temporary employment businesses. I believe I can take any business, even if I know nothing about it, and I can make it better. The first thing you ask yourself about the opportunity is: *"Is there a market for the product?"* I like to establish that there is a market for a product. And then I ask, *"Do you think you can do it properly? Do you think you can make your product for that market properly?"*

One other thing: as far as dot-com companies, I don't have a feel for those kinds of businesses. When the dot-com craze hit, I didn't jump in. I wouldn't put a nickel into that. I can't see it, can't touch it, and it's a gamble that people would advertise on the sites. It's just not my kind of deal. Maybe I'm old-fashioned or shortsighted but you can't be good at everything. Just about the time you think you're successful, you see some kid worth $80 billion and you say, *"Holy s---, here I am, I've worked all my life, growing companies and developing products, and I can't even approach that."*

Finding your opportunity

I think leveraged buyouts are a tremendous opportunity, and the reason I do them is because you get to use the bank's money, and they do most of the buying of the deal, and yet you get all the benefits. All you have to do is pay interest on the money. Now if it goes down, you lose your investment, but you get all the upside of it — and what a deal. I can show you over and over how I've done it. I think LBOs are a much easier way for a guy without money to earn millions compared to a new venture.

Another thing I want to tell you is you never know where a deal's going to come from. You never know. You to keep your ears open and be opportunistic. There's no pattern.

Royal Appliance. After I was running Invacare for about two years, a person I had worked with at another company came to me with an opportunity to buy Royal Appliance Manufacturing

Co., a Cleveland company later best known for its Dirt Devil vacuum cleaners. The former colleague asked if I would help him buy the company. I had purchased Invacare not that much earlier, so I didn't have any money. I didn't have a dollar.

He was looking at a $4 million price. I said, *"I'll do this for you. I'll put a deal together."* Essentially, it was a copy of the Invacare deal. I offered this deal to the same investors who invested in Invacare with me. Half said yes, and half said no. Somebody asked, *"What the hell do you know about vacuum cleaners? How do you go from wheelchairs to vacuum cleaners?"* I said, *"I don't know much about them, but it sounds like a good opportunity."* I've never been afraid to learn something new. I may not know about it, but I can learn enough about it to be dangerous, as the saying goes.

Many of the investors in Invacare, probably more than half, didn't want to be in. But I went ahead. I sat with this guy next to me and negotiated the deal with the seller, an older German fellow. In some ways, the interesting thing was that he thought marketing was some kind of a disease. He wouldn't touch it. Royal Appliance was the oldest vacuum-cleaner company in America — founded in 1905, and hardly anyone had ever heard of it. These were metal vacuum cleaners, and they were all sold through vacuum cleaner shops.

Ours was not the highest offer on the table; another offer was a little more money. But the owner sold it to us because the other bidder was a strategic buyer who was going to shut it down and take it out of state. The owner was very loyal to his people and to Ohio. I don't know who the other bidder was, but we got the company because we were going to keep it.

We paid $4 million for the company. On the inventory, receivables and equipment, we were able to get a loan that provided $1.25 million of the $4 million. Then we did a sale leaseback of the building for $1.4 million. The company had cash in it to provide working capital, but we used $1.1 million of that cash to buy it. Finally, the shareholders put up $100,000 of subordinated debt. I didn't have to take that loan. There was also $150,000 of common stock.

So if you add all those up — $1.25 million loan from the bank, $1.4 million from the sale leaseback, $1.1 million in cash from the company, $100,000 subordinated debt — we really only bought the company for the $150,000 of stock and the $100,000 of subordinated debt.

Now, I put the deal together, and in return, what I got out of it was a note from the company for $20,000. Because the sale of the stock was $150,000 and there was also $50,000 in notes, there was really $200,000 of equity if you cap the notes.

So we bought a $4 million company for $200,000 of equity and $100,000 in a subordinated note. That is — $300,000!

Here is my part of it. I didn't have any money, and I put the deal together, so as I said they loaned me (payable at $2,000 a year for 10 years) $20,000 for 10 percent of the company. I didn't have to put any money up and with our notes plus the stock that they paid cash for, the total common stock was $200,000. So I had 10 percent of it in a $20,000 note; in effect, I put no money into it. I paid $2,000 a year for 10 years. Then I got about $30 million on the IPO. Soon after we bought Royal, I ended up with 12 percent of it. One operator-investor had a falling out with the CEO and left the company. The company had enough cash to buy back the principal's stock, and I got some of those additional shares.

Now get this: The company's sales representatives at that time were each older than 65 years of age. I didn't know that. Can you believe a group of retired people selling the product? It was like a side job, sort of like, *"Well, we'll give you something to do in your retirement."* They sold the machines through vacuum cleaner shops. The Royal sales people just walked up to a vacuum cleaner shop and asked, *"Will you take my line?"*

The first thing we did was offer a real incentive plan for the sales force, a dynamic and ambitious plan. When I announced this program, there wasn't a single smile on their faces. Not a smile. That was the point at which I figured out they were all 65 and over and were concerned that if they made bonus money it would interfere with their Social Security checks.

I thought I was doing a good thing. And I said, *"Gee, I can't believe this."* So those who wanted to stayed and those who didn't left. We got busy developing and marketing. We launched a handheld plastic vacuum cleaner named the Dirt Devil Hand Vac. Lois Wyse of Wyse Advertising came up with the Dirt Devil name. We decided on a red color, and the first retail store we sold to was Higbee's, at that time a popular Cleveland department store. Then we hired veteran ABC Radio Networks broadcaster Paul Harvey to push the product, which was really an amazing thing. He started his regular news/commentary programs with something like, *"Hello Americans, I'm Paul Harvey. You know what the news is, and in a minute, you're going to hear ... the rest of the story,"* and ended it, *"This is Paul Harvey ... Good day!"*

Harvey started talking about this little American company in Ohio, right in the heart of the United States, and he talked how great this product was, made by Americans. All of a sudden, the phones rang off the hook. He got us really going. And then we started this massive TV spot buy, and Walmart and

Kmart got on board and the thing exploded. We were a private company, so we were able to sneak up on Hoover, which was a public company. They didn't know what was happening. That's one of the benefits of being a private company. No one can get at your financial information because it is private.

Near the end of our ownership, there was a lawyer who called me to his house. He told me that the CEO planned to take Royal Appliance public. Meanwhile, this had not been discussed with the board — and I'm chairman of the company. The lawyer told me, *"We're going to take the company public. There's going to be a board shakeup, and I would like you to stay on the board, but we're going to replace some board members."* I let him go on and tell me all this.

Finally, I said, *"You know, what you say is really interesting stuff, but, you know, I'm from Oklahoma, and I don't know a lot about this going public stuff, you know?"* At that time, Invacare was not yet public, but I said, *"You know, I thought that whoever controlled the company made those kinds of decisions."* He said, *"That's right. That's right. Your colleague controls it."* I told him, *"Why don't you go back and do your homework and you check and I'll check, because I think I control the company,"* which I did. The CEO didn't have enough votes. They were all my buddies that were in the deal, and I said, *"Now, I think I control the company. And if I don't, then ignore what I'm about to tell you, but I'm going to tell you that I don't have any problem taking the company public."*

"But," I said, *"You're not going to take us public. The attorney for the company when we bought the company will be taking us public. The day we go public, the day afterward, you can be the lawyer, but the other attorney is going to be the lawyer up to that point."*

Next, I told him that the board would remain as it was until we went public, and then the next day, he could do anything he wanted with the board — he could be the attorney of record then.

"I'm going to tell you what," I said. *"I'm going to resign that day and I won't be on the board."* And that's what happened. He checked and found out that the CEO didn't control the company. The day we went public, I resigned from the board. As for the other board members, some of them stayed on, but a lot didn't. The CEO and this lawyer put some other people on the board; I never looked back.

Later, I don't want to be critical of my ex-colleague, but he lost the company. He resigned. A Hong Kong company eventually purchased it.

The $30 million I realized out of the IPO when Royal went public was where I really got some cash in my hands. It allowed me to buy and do some things without selling any of Invacare. For instance, I created the first chair in entrepreneurship, the A. Malachi Mixon III Professor of Entrepreneurial Studies, at the Weatherhead School of Management at Case Western Reserve University.

I had to pay a lot of income tax from the proceeds, but it allowed me to get my ranch in Texas, my house in Florida and a little spending money here and there.

STERIS. I'm going to tell you about a deal that didn't cost a nickel and I made several million dollars. But it was the hardest matter I've ever been involved with. All my money was tied up in Invacare so I had to look elsewhere, and for me, a completely new venture was very difficult to do.

I met with J.B. Richey and a banker friend at Nighttown Restaurant in Cleveland Heights. There was a man named Lou Swartz whom we hired to find investment opportunities for us. We paid him a salary, it wasn't much, and he found these entrepreneurs who had the idea to make a sterilization machine to sterilize endoscopes — and not just disinfect them.

At that time, a company called American Sterilizer took the used endoscopes and sterilized them overnight. They had a virtual monopoly on the process. Because the process took so long to sterilize them and used the flammable gas ethylene oxide, they had to deal with the FDA and the EPA. Needless to say, it was a hell of a complicated procedure. Only the first person in the morning got a sterilized instrument. Then they'd dip these endoscopes in disinfectant tanks all day long.

When AIDS came along, I started thinking to myself, *"I wouldn't want something stuck in me that isn't sterilized, you know."* I asked people including a doctor, *"Would you rather have a sterilized instrument or a disinfected instrument?"* The doctor said, *"Mixon, what kind of question is that, for God's sake? Of course, I'd rather have a sterilized instrument, but you can't sterilize it for every procedure. It takes four hours or something like that."* And I said, *"OK, would you rather have a sterilized instrument for less money than a disinfected instrument costs you?"* He said, *"Are you crazy? You're asking me would I rather have sterilized over disinfected for less money."* Well, that's what the concept was. We aimed to deliver a sterilized endoscope cheaper than hospitals were paying to disinfect endoscopes.

J.B. Richey was interested in it from a technical point of view. I asked him, *"Do you think this'll work?"* *"Yeah,"* he said, *"I think it'll work."* I said, *"OK, I like it."* I didn't care how it worked as long as it did, and we could deliver sterilized equipment cheaper than disinfected ones. As long as J.B. knew how it worked, that was fine with me.

I've often told the story that after dinner at Nighttown, amid the smooth jazz that was being performed, I decided we'd do an incubator. I approached Loyal Wilson, CEO of Primus Capital Funds. He didn't think it would work, but he didn't want to insult me because I was on the board of Primus, so he hired Bill Sanford, then president of Symark Associates, to do a study to prove that my idea was a dumb one. But Sanford countered, *"It's a great idea. I'd like to be the CEO."*

Wilson decided to invest, and I think it took $20 million before one sale was made. Obviously, I couldn't fund that. Invacare put some money in it, and I got a little stock for putting the deal together. We built a prototype and got some grant money from the state and called it STERIS, a play on the word sterilize. The deal was done with mostly venture capital money. I think Invacare made several million dollars out of the thing, and I started The Invacare Foundation with the profits we made on STERIS. It is now a public company.

The real story about STERIS to me is that after we took it public, the stock went so high that the company did a reverse Pac-Man acquisition and actually bought American Sterilizer. I say reverse Pac-Man because the company, this big sterilization company, rejected the original idea, and it cost the CEO his company. I didn't join the STERIS board because I thought that Sanford was a lot like me, a marketing guy. J.B. went on the board. The company needed to develop the product, and he stayed on the board a long time and contributed to getting the product developed, perfected and so forth. J.B. used to squirt water all over the place trying to get the thing to work. How do you sterilize endoscopes? It was interesting — it's kind of a washing machine, really.

But I didn't really care about the process. I let J.B. worry about that; I was sold on the idea of a sterilized instrument for less money.

A different approach — MCM Capital Partners
By the mid-1980s and early 1990s, my reputation for doing well as an investor led people to start presenting opportunities to me. A lot of them weren't worth the paper they were written on, but I had to go through them all to see if any were worth developing.

That's when we created MCM Capital Partners, which stands for Mixon, Callahan and Mansour. These are my very close friends, and we have invested together going all the way back to the Invacare deal. F. Joseph Callahan was the CEO of Swagelok Co., and Ernie Mansour was the managing partner of a prominent Cleveland law firm and has also done legal work for me.

Making investments deal by deal by deal was getting to be tough. I knew I needed a better way. I said to myself, *"I'm tired of having to raise this damn money every time. Why not raise a clump of money, say $50 million, and then I won't have to worry about it?"* That's how MCM came about. With MCM, if we found an opportunity, we had a ready source for the investment money. We usually didn't want to put more than $5 million in a deal so we affiliated with other venture companies when a larger deal came along. They'd kind of scratch your back and you'd scratch theirs. … It's sort of an incestuous industry — you're really not a competitor with a venture company. They all eat at the same buffet.

Ernie's son, Mark, who was an auditor with Price Waterhouse, had done some investment work and got my attention. I told Mark my idea for a capital fund and flat out asked him to run it. He agreed, and he's built a hell of a company now. There have been two fundraisings at MCM, each about $50 million. We've made deals for at least nine companies.

We did OK on the first fundraising. But the second fundraising was unbelievable. We have six companies now in the fund, and they're all doing well. MCM is performing in the top 10 percent of all venture capital funds in the country. I think before all the results are in, and we sell off all these companies, we'll be in the top 5 percent. I give Mark the credit, not me. He's a very good manager.

As for the kind of structure of MCM, it limited itself to leveraged buyouts of manufacturing companies. So some of my later deals, such as for Air Enterprises and Encore Bank, weren't eligible to receive MCM's assistance.

Opportunity keeps knocking

Wilshire Corp. This next deal is one of which I am very proud. It was excellent — because I bought the company with zero money. I was walking my dog on a Sunday afternoon, and I ran into my lawyer friend Bob Gudbranson. He said, *"Mal, I had a deal for a company, and the principal just backed out. I need somebody to step in who can do this deal." "What's the deal?"* I asked. He said, *"Well, first of all, you've got to buy the plant for $2 million, and you have to buy $1 million in receivables. That's $3 million. And you've got to put in $330,000 equity, and the equity will give you 23 percent of the deal."*

So I said, *"Let me go over and talk to Joe Callahan."* It was still Sunday, and I went over to Callahan's. We talked it through, I called my banker that night, and in no time, I had $2 million as a sale-leaseback part of the deal. I didn't need to buy the plant. Then, I looked at the receivables, which totaled $1.4 million from blue-chip customers such as Coca-Cola and Kentucky Fried Chicken.

What was the product? It was Wilshire dispensing valves for beverage-making machines. We put them in McDonald's and so on. The client list was like a *"Who's Who"* of the restaurant franchise world. I took a million-dollar bank loan guaranteed by the $1.4 million in receivables. I borrowed the $330,000 that we put in equity. So I got $400,000 for my receivables. I used that money to fund the equity.

Bob Gudbranson, my lawyer friend, sent me a memo on the Wilshire deal in which he assessed the entire deal:

"A review of this transaction and the ultimate sale by Wilshire Partners can be summarized by saying there was a spectacular return on investment. The original equity of approximately $1 million resulted in a total sale price of $39.8 million contributing a 40-to-1 return on equity."

I went on the board of that company. We built a hell of a great company and had a lot of fun. Eventually, we sold it. Isn't that a great story?

Cencor Temporary Services. The CEO of a Kansas City public company passed away, and in order to pay the taxes on his estate, his widow had to sell a subsidiary called Cencor Temporary Services. I learned about the matter from my accountant. This company had temporary employment offices all over Ohio. I purchased the Ohio division of the company, but I didn't know anything about temporary employment. I think we put in $400,000 in total equity and made several million dollars out of that deal, all because I was willing to listen to an opportunity and take a calculated risk.

While I didn't feel I knew much about the *"temping"* business, I did know a lot about salesmanship. I started working my relationships in Cleveland, and I got a lot of business as a result. I took the approach, *"Who would use temporary employment among my network of business contacts?"* My partners and I did a good job, and we kept building it. Any time one of my businesses or contacts needed temporary workers, we'd call Cencor. Then a public company came along that was planning to do a national rollup, and it wanted to buy Cencor. The company offered us some ridiculous price, and we agreed. We sold it for $13.5 million. About $11 million went to shareholders — there was a debt on the books obviously, but it was another great deal.

Air Enterprises. One more great story is that of Air Enterprises. The company, which manufactures aluminum air-handling systems, had filed for bankruptcy in April 2005. We bought it out of bankruptcy. Bill Weber and I purchased it for $2.75 million in partnership with Resilience Capital Partners, a Cleveland fund that buys distressed companies.

We paid Resilience a 100 percent premium within a year for the balance of the company. Weber was running it, and I was an equal partner. Among our customers were Pfizer, Eli Lilly, Case Western Reserve University and hospitals, including the Cleveland Clinic.

Along came an order from Massachusetts General Hospital, something involving a $5 million bonding guarantee. Resilience didn't want to guarantee the deal and didn't want to pay for a bond. So it took a quick profit of 100 percent. Because of my assets at that time, I was able to make the guarantee. Mass General wasn't going to give us the order unless we bonded it. To my way of thinking, it was a big step that we took. And it's grown from no backlog to where we have a $30 million backlog.

When you get down to it, what Air Enterprises is trying to do is sell energy savings, not equipment. When you install our systems, they're the very best in the world. They don't have much air leakage, and even though the equipment costs more, it saves energy. We make them out of aluminum instead of steel — all of the old steel systems have rusted out. We created a product line called SiteBilt, where we replace these old steel systems on site and build an air handling system. After filing for bankruptcy, the company had about 60 employees. Today, we employ more than 250 people.

Encore National Bank. I have been traveling to Naples, Fla., for 20 years, and I had been looking for opportunities there. But I never found any because they were all real estate or restaurant, and I couldn't find anything to get my teeth into.

Finally, I developed a friendship with a fellow, and he found out about a bank in Houston, Texas. It was a public company that was going to get rid of its Florida operations because banks were getting in trouble at that time due to the economy. They had to write down their bad loans. Let's say that a bank is worth $20 million book value. You have to write some bad loans down to $10 million book value. Then you write off some more loans, and it's down to $5 million book value. The Fed makes you raise some more equity, or you'll have to close the bank. So the way you raise equity was to sell off the assets of loans and deposits in an area. This bank had already written it down, so anything it got was a premium. Well, I was in. We paid a little bit for deposits and loans and the bank could raise equity that way. I put all the bad loans back to the parent companies and all I kept were the good loans.

I didn't know much about banking, but it sounded like a good opportunity. I've never been afraid to learn something new. When I do something like that, I try to accomplish it with people who know what they're doing. For Encore Bank, I have people involved who invested in banks all their lives. Those are the kinds of people you need when you are in a highly regulated industry.

So we started the bank. My investors were primarily from Cleveland. We bought four branches of a bank in Naples and a single branch bank that had a national charter. We put the four branches into this bank and made five branches: Naples, North Naples, Fort Meyers, Port Charlotte and Tampa. Recently, the government approved the purchases of two new branches. But, it occurred to me that if I had a bank, it should be very accommodating to the local businesses in southwest Florida that we'd focus on the business market and the known professionals. If you go into our branch, it looks like a club. It doesn't look like a bank. It's real friendly and warm and TVs are all around. You don't feel like you're in a bank. Our whole goal is to be very friendly — and we loan money. We've got millions of dollars to loan because we've got more deposits and equity than loans. We're one of the few Florida banks that aren't in trouble. So, it's pretty small, relative to other banks, but we haven't lost $4 billion on trading, derivatives or anything risky like that.

We plan to acquire other branches and build a really good bank in southwest Florida, so someday a bigger bank is going to come and say, *"Geez, I want to be over there in southwest Florida."* That's my goal. Who knows how it's going to work out?

Get yourself a jockey, money and an exit strategy

After you find your opportunity, probably the most important thing is to have a jockey who can ride the horse (the horse, of course, is the business). But if you get a blockhead, forget it. It's never going to work. And a good man, a good woman — a good person — can make lemonade out of a lemon usually, even if the market or the opportunity is not as good as you thought.

If you have a good jockey, you're going to be successful. If you have a bad jockey, even if you have a tremendous opportunity, you aren't going to achieve your goals. So you've got to spend time to take a serious look at and make a judgment about the person who leads the business.

One other very, very important thing, of course, is money. Most deals that fail do so because the entrepreneur didn't have enough money to do it. And when I say money, just the initial money isn't always enough. The point is, don't do a deal if you haven't figured out how you're going to get the money throughout the business cycle.

You can have a damn good idea, but if you don't have the money to execute it, you're just not going to carry it out. But a bank loan is money, too. I didn't have much capital in Invacare, but I had a sizable bank loan. The point is you have to plan the financial part of your deal and know what you're going to do and how you're going to get the money.

Lastly, have an exit strategy: *"I'm going to do this and I want to sell it in five years. I want to take it public."* Don't perpetuate the thinking, *"I'm going to turn it over to my children."* Well, why would anyone invest in that, you know? If you're going to keep it in the family for 200 years, I'll never be able to cash out.

It's important that you have a buyable strategy. As I've told investors when we were buying a bank, we ought to have a five-to seven-year outlook. By five to seven years, I hope to sell the bank to a bigger bank. In general, seven years is the optimum time to cash in and then sell.

One venture that hit a brick wall

Of all my investments, many have been successful but not all of them. Here is the story of a company that I started that I think was ahead of its time, and due to several circumstances, it didn't make it.

With financial help from Invacare, Primus Ventures, Morganthaler Ventures and other sources, I was able to raise some $20 million for a startup company called NeuroControl. This was in the late 1990s, and a technology called functional electrical stimulation (FES) came on the scene. My group wanted to commercialize it. It was pretty revolutionary for the time: A small computerized implant would send signals to the arms and hands of a quadriplegic so he or she would be able to grasp objects — so the person could dress or eat and so forth.

We actually sold several million dollars worth of the devices. The system did work but the market was too small and many physicians would not prescribe the device. This, combined with a long delay in gaining marketing approval from the FDA, caused us to run out of money. Today, FES has successfully been applied in other areas.

Basically, I thought it was a sound medical thing that we were doing. It was very high-tech stuff, but we had our hands full trying to push this technology. I asked Donna Richardson to step in as CEO. She was looking for an opportunity for a technology to be further developed and had been working as a consultant at NeuroControl. She worked very hard to turn the company around — and actually improved sales from $1 million a year to $5 million and employment from 12 to 60. But it still wasn't enough.

I will let Donna tell the story.

Thanks, Mal, I get to be the one in your book that didn't make it! Why can't I be one of the ones that was a success? Ha! Ha!

But we worked very, very hard at NeuroControl, and I learned a great deal from Mal. When I first started, everything was broken. We had an FDA situation, we had a supplier issue, reimbursement was not in place, we didn't have a good sales team, and we had to re-furb all that.

It was one of those opportunities that nobody wanted to see stopped — an implantable neural stimulation device for spinal injured C-5/C-6 patients. The patient population is truly traumatized and usually unintentionally: swimming pool accidents, car accidents, skiing. The victims are usually young people and are very disabled. The opportunity to bring some technology that would allow them more function in their lives was very intoxicating for the investors and the management team and for the excellent technology team.

I think Mal kind of summed it up: We were probably 20 years ahead of our time from a technology standpoint. New devices are being developed that are much more technically advanced, and they give patients more function.

One of the problems was reimbursement. For any kind of long-term implantable medical device, it is always a challenge because these patients usually don't have insurance. What we managed to get reimbursed with a lot of effort worked out. The issue was patients who once they had an injury like this — they are very, very reluctant to have any kind of procedure performed that would force them to have rehab for a couple of months or the period of time that it would take for recovery.

The physicians that care for them are very reluctant to recommend this to patients because these patients will live a normal life span of 70 years — it's just that they need constant care. We did do a couple hundred of patients, but NeuroControl couldn't get a revenue ramp beyond $5 million.

We would spend four or five months trying to get these patients ready for the surgery, the surgeon lined up, and we would have to pay for their travel to the hospital, for the various evaluations, and then they get a urinary tract infection or decubitus ulcers returned — so you'd have to cancel the surgery. It was a very difficult market to manage.

We couldn't get there with the money we had. While we raised $15 million, we realized that we were going to have to downsize. We decided to get out of the spinal cord product and just focus on the stroke product. That was in October 2001.

For the three years that I ran the company, the staff focused on spinal cord injuries.

Once we realized that we couldn't get a revenue ramp out of the spinal cord product, we shut that down, and we brought the stroke product forward and cut the company down to about 20 people. That's when I left because there was no reason for me to stay on. It was just going to be a little R&D group.

Invacare supported it as an R&D project for a couple of millions of dollars a year. J.B. Richey was still the chairman, and they kept the R&D stroke product going for another three or four years.

When FDA delays seemed endless, that's when Invacare decided it could no longer afford to support the project. They completely shut it down.

But throughout, what I found so inspiring about Mal was that he rolls up his sleeves, and he works with you. He doesn't dominate, he doesn't take over, but he has a really terrific ability to naturally guide you, lead you and is always inspiring.

I remember one time talking about some things before a board meeting or something, and I said, "This is where we have weaknesses in this area." He said, "Donna, we don't have any weaknesses. We have challenges." I said, "Yes, you're right." And I always do that now in business. He is absolutely right. We have particular challenges and we have to find solutions for them. You don't feel you're taking risks when you are working with Mal. He is so inspiring with his confidence that things can happen in a can-do way, you realize we can make this happen; that's how I worked with him.

What would have helped NeuroControl to survive?

First of all, the patient population was one that no one wanted to give up on. The team that I had assembled was a terrific team. I think my leadership also, much of that inspired by Mal, was a key factor, so people didn't want to give up. This was one of those circumstances where we should've shut it down sooner. I think everyone learns something. You fall in love with a particular situation, you are very passionate about it, a great deal of passion, and it takes a great deal of business discipline to realize no matter what we do, this isn't going to change.

That's really what that situation was. So we should have shut the spinal cord injury down sooner. Once we realized that the sales were just not going to be as robust as we needed them to be, we should have analyzed why each patient implant cost an enormous amount of money from the manufacturers' standpoint. We didn't have the margin from the business. Unless you have a patient population that has a much higher rate of implant, you're just not going to get there — and we just couldn't get there.

Epilogue on deal-making

When I look over my many deals, I find I earned my first million with the purchase of Invacare, but it was on paper only. I remember when I lived in Spiro, I thought if I could make $50-grand a year as an adult, I thought I'd have died and gone to heaven. That's $50,000 a year. It took cashing in Royal Appliance to even feel heavenly for a while. When I bought Royal Appliance, it gave me liquidity. When it comes to what's in your wallet, there are two things in life. There's net worth and there's liquidity. You can have a lot of net worth, but if you can't get at it, you can't spend it.

Invacare and Royal Appliance were both challenges for me because I had no money going into the deals. Before Invacare, I had no experience putting deals together. When I did the Royal deal, I had some experience, but I still didn't have any money.

I didn't have trouble selling myself or selling the deal. Getting the bank to lend money wasn't that hard to do. Royal was a much easier deal to make than Invacare; Invacare was tough. The bank wanted a life insurance policy on me, for Pete's sake. The equity portion was never hard to obtain for the Invacare deal because half the people I asked said yes and half said no; 50 percent is a pretty good batting average, I think. With Royal, I put the equity together so it was the bank loan that took some doing.

But after Invacare, putting deals together got easier. I had experience. I had a track record and word was getting around about my deal-making success.

I'm always waiting for my next deal. I'm waiting to find the next opportunity. That's really what I live for now. I'm not really ready to say, *"Well, I've made several million, so Barbara, let's clip coupons until we die."*

With the late Al Lerner, a retired Marine and once owner of the Cleveland Browns and USMC Gen. James L. Jones (ret.). Jones is on the Invacare Board of Directors.

My good friends, Dr. Floyd Loop, former CEO of the Cleveland Clinic, and his wife, the late Dr. Bernadine Healy, former head of the National Institutes of Health. "Bernie" served on the Invacare Board of Directors for a number of years.

Barb and Mal meet President George H. W. Bush.

Barb and Mal with President George W. Bush.

Dancing with daughter Elizabeth at the debutantes' ball.

Our son Ki and his bride Tasha and the Mixon family, 1997.

On the cover of "Small Business News", June 1995.

At an Invacare event: "Hello. I'm Mal Mixon."

Golfing with Invacare advertising spokesman Arnold Palmer and Ohio Gov. John Kasich, right.

Our daughter Elizabeth Mixon Ewig and from left, Katie, Trip, Liz, Charlie and Christian Malachi.

Our son Ki and his wife Tasha and Riley, left, and Aubrey (whose initials are AMM, like mine).

Debbie Warden, long-time executive assistant, and me at my Invacare office.

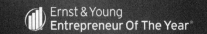

Ernst & Young
Entrepreneur Of The Year®

HEALTHY RETURNS

Mal Mixon has spent most of his life helping improve Northeast Ohio

A. Malachi (Mal) Mixon III is chairman of the board of Invacare Corp., a leading worldwide manufacturer and distributor of medical products for the home health care market. Mixon led a leveraged buyout of Invacare in 1979, when sales were $19 million. In 2009, Invacare was named to the *Fortune* 1000 and the *IndustryWeek* Manufacturing 500, and last year, the company achieved sales of $1.7 billion.

Mixon also serves on the public boards of The Sherwin-Williams Co. and Park-Ohio Holdings Corp. He also is a founding investor in MCM Capital Partners, a Cleveland leveraged buyout company. Additionally, he has been an active investor in several successful Cleveland-area ventures that became public companies, including Royal Appliance Manufacturing Co., creator of the "Dirt Devil" vacuum cleaner, and STERIS Corp., a world leader in medical sterilization products. He recently led the purchase of five bank branches in Florida that became Naples-based Encore National Bank.

A graduate of Leadership Cleveland, Mixon's current civic activities include serving as chairman emeritus of the board of directors and trustees of The Cleveland Clinic Foundation and chair of the Cleveland Institute of Music. In 2007, the institute opened Mixon Hall, a state-of-the-art performance hall. He also serves on the Visiting Committee of Harvard Business School and the board of MWV Pinnacle Capital Management, a fund investing in minority ventures. He has established a Mixon Scholarship in each new freshman class at Harvard College for students from Oklahoma and Northeast Ohio. Mixon also established a chair in entrepreneurial studies at the Weatherhead School of Management at Case Western Reserve University.

Originally from Oklahoma, Mixon is a graduate of Harvard College and Harvard Business School. Between degrees, he served four years in the U.S. Marine Corps, including a year in Vietnam, attaining the rank of captain. <<

HOW TO REACH: Invacare, www.invacare.com

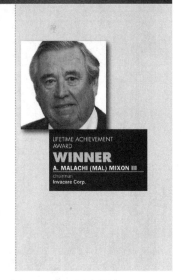

LIFETIME ACHIEVEMENT AWARD
WINNER
A. MALACHI (MAL) MIXON III
chairman
Invacare Corp.

Article from "Smart Business Northeast Ohio" magazine for the E&Y Lifetime Achievement Award, July 2011.

Exterior of Mixon Hall, Cleveland Institute of Music
(Mixon Hall photos courtesy of CIM/Leigh-Anne Dennison).

Interior of Mixon Hall.

Mixon Hall exterior view, showing the stage.

Views of the Admitting and Registration Room at the Cleveland Clinic heart center. Reprinted with permission, Cleveland Clinic Center for Medical Art & Photography © 2012. All Rights Reserved.

*Barbara and Mal by the fireplace,
circa late 1980s-early 1990s*

Barbara and Mal pose for a snapshot.

Enjoying the outdoors at a white-tie event.

One of our most recent photos (at Mixon Hall at CIM).

Chapter 9: The Stroke — and Giving Back

This all leads me into a natural transition about my most recent health challenge — my stroke. I was going through life hitting on all cylinders and feeling pretty good about life and myself. In April 2010, I took a business trip to Holland, and I woke up one morning — and I didn't know it, but I was having a stroke.

Looking around my hotel room, I felt a little disoriented. I thought maybe I had had too much to drink. After a few minutes, I took my shower, shaved, and at that point, I didn't have any impairment. Since I had a dinner meeting on my agenda, I figured I may as well attend even though I didn't feel very well. Gerry Blouch and Rob Gudbranson from Invacare and I were meeting with a team from Holland, and one of the group said he thought I slurred a couple of words, but nobody else noticed. The same afternoon we flew from Amsterdam to Geneva, and I had difficulty getting off the plane. We checked into a hotel.

All day long I was having a stroke, and I was not aware of it. I went to dinner with my team. I felt like hell. It was time to do something. I asked for help walking me to my hotel room. On the way, I started slurring my words, which is a sign of a stroke, so everyone was getting concerned. Someone was talking to Dr. Floyd Loop in Cleveland about every half hour about my condition. I remember that U.S. Rep. John Boehner called me, and I was slurring my words when I talked to him. I bet he thought I was drunk! He was the last person I talked to before I went to get medical attention in Geneva. Finally, Dr. Loop got someone to check me into the hospital. It was a teaching center called HUG, Hopitaux Universitaire de Geneve.

Things got worse. I couldn't move my left side. It was totally paralyzed. I think I stayed in bed for two or three days — it's all kind of a blur now. They put me through a CAT scanner and an MRI machine. After a while the hospital staff got me up and tried to get me to walk. I couldn't walk. My wife, Barb, and daughter, Elizabeth, flew over to see how I was doing.

I was a sick puppy in a foreign country. I had to wait 12 days in Switzerland before my plane could fly me back to Cleveland. We couldn't fly the normal route due to the volcanic ash in the atmosphere following an eruption in Iceland. We had to fly the southern route through Spanish airspace. Once in Cleveland, I checked into the neurological center at the Cleveland Clinic. I was there four or five weeks.

I went from a wheelchair to a walker to a cane to now walking without any assistance. I'm not by any stretch of the imagination healed yet, but I'm working like a son of a gun to get better. This has been the most difficult thing I have ever experienced. I went through Vietnam unscathed. The cancer that I had nowhere impaired me, physically, I mean. Maybe emotionally. This stroke impaired me physically. The struggle to bring myself back to where I can talk to someone today and play golf tomorrow was a lon-n-n-n-g trip back. I'm still a far piece from being normal again, but at least, I'm mobile. At first, I couldn't raise my arm. I couldn't even pick it up. It was just hanging, and I am left-handed to boot. I still can't write very well. I've learned to use my right hand. I get depressed once in a while, but I generally have been able to get back up and be positive about it.

Fortunately, unlike a lot of strokes, I don't think my brain was impaired; my speech was affected a little bit but not enough for doctors to recommend that I go through speech training. I went to the Cleveland Clinic's W.O. Walker Center for therapy for more that two years. I have a physical therapist come to my house twice a week.

The Clinic staff had me write down what I wanted to do. They wanted to encourage me to strive for activities. I said I wanted to jog — they didn't say I couldn't jog either! The thing that they haven't said to me is, *"That's as good as you're going to get."* I guess in the early days they said, *"Stroke? You're impaired. That's it."* Now they are finding that while the recovery is slower as you go farther away from the event, you can still recover.

I decided to relinquish the chairmanship of the Cleveland Clinic board, and then I decided to relinquish the CEO job at Invacare. I'm still chairman of the board. In terms of physical activity, I used to play the piano a lot, and I really enjoyed quail hunting on my ranch in Texas. I was a crack shot, not just with a shotgun. In the Marine Corps, I was an expert at pistol and at rifle — they are totally two different types of shooting but are all hand-and-eye coordination.

Anyway, the stroke really slowed me down. But I've tried hunting two years in a row. I'm getting better. The main problem now is walking for me on uneven terrain. I can hold a gun up. I can't turn quite as adeptly as I did before, and I used to be able to shoot over my head and that sort of thing.

Another thing is that impairment affects your fun time, too. I enjoy sports, and I enjoy watching football and that sort of thing so I can still do that. I like just about anything. I've tried a lot of different things, and I can have fun almost doing something simple. I play golf, and I've enjoyed golf not because I was very good but I enjoy the outdoors.

I could have easily said I am through, I am retiring to be a housemother, but I am trying to take the high road, I have really tried, and some days, it's pretty tough. You get up, and it's always a bit of a struggle.

Beyond that, I have pretty well kept my other activities. I was in a daze for a while, but it is a very difficult thing to go through. I don't smoke. I don't think I am vastly overweight and I am pretty active physically. I never dreamed that it would happen to me. I don't remember anyone in my family ever having a stroke.

My advice as a result of my stroke would be to be sure you aren't overweight and that you eat the right things and do the right things because I thought I was invincible up to that point. Your life is not going to go in a straight line. You are going to have setbacks. And you've got to have the strength to get through the tough times, not the easy times. Anybody can enjoy the easy times.

I wish I hadn't had the stroke because I've dreamed of having a good time in my retirement. But I am making the best of it.

I have made a few investments since my stroke. I put the bank together in Florida. I am always on the lookout for opportunities, and I enjoy being busy. I enjoy handling a variety of different challenges and problems; it keeps me busy. And Barbara is happy.

Giving back

I think as you get older, you tend — maybe after you've accomplished a few things in life — to think about other people. The point is it's important to give back — and not just make money. That's why I started my philanthropy efforts.

One of the facets of my career has been about acknowledging the little guy and his or her value of what he or she brings to the table. My attitude was that I want to help the kids who were like me — I made my money in Northeast Ohio. Why do I donate to institutions? It's because I feel like it's my town. It's where I made my money, and I want to give back to that community. I'm not bragging about giving money away. It isn't because I want to brag, or I feel it's an obligation. I just want to do it. Barbara and I have talked it over and the thought of giving something after you were dead doesn't do much for me. I really enjoy giving now.

Bernadine Healy, physician and a former head of the National Institutes of Health as well as the American Red Cross, told me one time, *"Mal, you can't fit it in the casket, you know. You've got to do something with it while you're still alive."*

The thing I am proudest of was being chairman of the Cleveland Clinic board of trustees for 13 years. I was elected to the board in 1992 and appointed to serve on the executive committee of the board of trustees. In 1997, I was named chairman of the board and served until 2010. In 2009, the executive committee was recast and became the board of directors, which currently serves as the fiduciary board of The Cleveland Clinic Foundation.

While I was at the helm, the Clinic had unprecedented growth and service. The Clinic opened the Sydell and Arnold Miller Pavilion (the heart center) and the Glickman Tower (the urology and kidney center), the groundbreaking in Abu Dhabi, and the opening of the Lou Ruvo Center for Brain Health in Las Vegas.

It's been a labor of love because I have learned a lot about medicine and medical things. Of course, I am in that industry, but I've really made a lot of great friends. That was one of the pleasures of my life.

The Cleveland Clinic has grown from 300 to 3,000 doctors in my career. The Clinic made me chairman emeritus in December 2010.

My first gift to the Clinic went to the Miller Family Pavilion (the heart center) and is named the Barbara and Mal Mixon, Gayle and J.B. Richey and Invacare Corp. Registration and Admitting area. A second gift went toward the Cole Eye Institute where the doctors and nurses saved my eyesight. I had something called a macular hole, not a disease, a physical thing in which as you get older, your eye shrinks a bit, pulls away from the retina and sometimes it creates a hole. I had it in both eyes. If you don't take care of it, this black hole just keeps getting bigger and bigger and pretty soon you can't see. But anyway, they fixed my eyes and I thought I would do something for the institute and Dr. Daniel Martin, chairman. I sponsored his endowed chair in ophthalmology, the Barbara and A. Malachi Mixon, III Institute Chair in Ophthalmology.

In 2007, the new Mixon Hall opened at the Cleveland Institute of Music. Barbara and I gave a $3 million gift to fund the hall. People who attend concerts there are really impressed. It's very small, 235 seats, and the acoustics are incredible. They can change the baffling to accommodate the sound waves of an opera singer, pianist, violinist or whatever it is. You can hear a pin drop; the acoustics are that good. They tell me it's the finest performing hall in the world. It employs all the latest techniques and the latest theories about sound waves.

In 1997, I established a Mixon Scholarship for a student in each new freshman class at Harvard College. This is for a youth from either Oklahoma or Northeast Ohio. Every year, the Mixon Scholarship student writes to tell me what he or she is doing. One year a girl from Enid, Okla., became a Rhodes Scholar on my scholarship, and that made me feel really good that I contributed to get this girl through school from Oklahoma — but anyway, these kids, they tell me about their background and what they're doing. In a lot of cases, they come from families with no money, like I did, and I feel pretty good about that.

Another thing I'm proud of is that I helped start MWV (Minorities With Vision) Pinnacle Capital Management. As I got older, I began to have more social conscience about trying to affect my community for the good. It all stemmed from my view that to solve Cleveland's problems in the inner city — they're going to be solved by minorities, not by whites. What we need is more black wealth. They're concerned about their community, and they go back in. That's really what we need. So I got interested in, *"Well, how do we create some black wealth?"* I started this fund with the first million dollars. I talked Dan Moore into putting money in; I got Sherwin-Williams, my other contacts, and the banks involved. I think we raised about $25 million.

The idea was that a minority person would run it. It would have no strings attached, no government funds, none of those handouts. The cash was to help minority businesses start, expand, launch new product lines or acquire other companies. For some cases, the fund may purchase local firms itself and install minority managers.

We looked for young entrepreneurs, minority entrepreneurs who would give back, or we'd buy a business and restructure it to have a minority control. Well, we've done that, and we've been mildly successful. The fund is out of money now, and we need a second round of investment.

Lest I overlook them, I've also been a director of a number of companies listed on the New York Stock Exchange, including the Sherwin-Williams Co., Lamson & Sessions Co. and Park-Ohio.

I gave the first half-million dollars to help start the National Museum of the Marine Corps near Quantico, Va., and it's a beautiful museum. They've had more than 2 million visitors. My name's the first one on the plaque. I gave money when it was a risk; it was an idea, and it was questionable whether enough money could be raised. Marines came out of the woodwork all over the country. They raised $40 million to $50 million before construction was started. I think they've raised more than $75 million now. I'm proud of providing the seed money that got the thing off the ground. I did that because of my love for the Marine Corps, and I wanted to perpetuate its history.

I funded the first entrepreneurship chair at the Case Western Reserve University Weatherhead School of Management. That was with some of my profits from the Royal Appliance deal.

J.B. Richey and I donated $5 million to the Case School of Engineering at Case Western Reserve University to fund The Richey-Mixon Building. It's called *"The Think Box."* It will house inventors and entrepreneurs, and we're going to try to spawn more Cleveland businesses. We hope that lawyers and investment bankers and other people would want to be in the building. It will have the resources the entrepreneurs need. J.B. and I, when we retire, plan to have our offices there. I'm pretty excited about the concept.

The main reason I committed to this was that by working with J.B. on it, I hope we can help the next generation of young people with vision to take some risks and do some things in Cleveland. The idea is to help other young entrepreneurs who have good ideas but no money. I think with young entrepreneurs, I enjoy somebody who's got similar drive who doesn't have any money. They've got a lot of drive, a lot of talent, a lot of those qualities. I enjoy seeing them succeed. It's nice making money, but I get my kicks now out of helping somebody else succeed.

Chapter 10: When Mal's Out of the Office ...

When I look back at my experiences, I realize how they have helped me become a successful entrepreneur. While many, if not most of the stories that I have recounted, relate to business matters, let me assure everyone that all work and no play is not part of the Mixon credo. I have many hobbies and pastimes outside of work. Much of Barbara's and my time goes to philanthropy, which I have already described. But I enjoy getting away from it all. For instance, I used to play the piano a lot, but my stroke has kind of put a damper on that. I'm pretty good at shooting craps. I like country music, especially singers Willie Nelson, Garth Brooks and others. In Alaska, I've had some great fishing trips with my friends.

Around 10 years ago, I bought Elm Creek, my ranch in Texas, about an hour and a half from Amarillo, from business magnate and financier T. Boone Pickens. My friends and I hunt quail, occasionally wild turkey, usually five to six hours a day, and there are also deer and boar. The boars get up to 300-400 pounds quickly and are mean as hell. I let a trapper trap them, and he sells the meat.

We ride horses sometimes and have a good time. Hunting season starts in October each year and we haven't missed opening weekend yet, even after I had my stroke. I have a ranch manager who lives on the property and maintains it. He and his wife are some of the finest people I know.

I've always had a great love of sports. I am a big fan of Oklahoma college football and, of course, all the Cleveland teams. I try to get to most games here — I have a box at Progressive Field, Cleveland Browns Stadium and Quicken Loans Arena for the Cavs. If I am not at a game, I can always find a game on TV worth watching.

A number of years ago, some friends and I put in a bid to buy the Cleveland Browns. We didn't get the team, but I'm glad the buyer kept the Browns in Cleveland.

What's in a name?

I have received numerous awards over the years so it's a real chore to keep the list current. Rather than attempt to list them all, suffice it to say that there are many, many of them, and I am deeply honored having received them all. Two stand out in my mind: In 2007, I received the Harvard Business School Alumni Achievement Award, the school's highest honor, and in 2011, I received the Lifetime Achievement Award in the Ernst & Young Entrepreneur Of The Year Awards in Northeast Ohio.

While my donations and awards give my name some staying power, the recognition is not a big thing to me. As I said earlier, I'd rather give back while I am still alive. Which brings me another point — after my son (he's Aaron Malachi Mixon IV), there won't be any more Aaron Malachi Mixons to carry on the name. It doesn't particularly bother me. Nope. My granddaughters make me proud — and one, Aubrey, actually has the AMM initials.

As for my family, Barbara and I have two children, as I said, Elizabeth and Ki (which is short for Malachi), and six grandchildren. Elizabeth has four children, three boys and a girl, and they live in New Jersey. My son and his wife have two daughters. They are all healthy, and they're good, smart kids. Their girls go to Hathaway Brown School, which is where Barbara and my daughter went; they are our third generation of Hathaway Brown girls. Barbara and I sponsored the new playground there. If you go by Hathaway Brown, you have to see the playground. It's out of this world. Barbara is on the board at the school.

I am proud of my son for making his own career and not doing it on his daddy's nickel. We have an anti nepotism rule at Invacare, so Ki never worked for Invacare. Instead, he is a partner of Resilience Capital Partners, which is a firm that buys bankrupt companies. He's really done a hell of a job. He went to night school at the Case Western Reserve University Weatherhead School of Management. He worked on a rotation through McDonald & Co., and he met some colleagues and left with them when they started Resilience.

I'm grateful for such a wonderful family, and I feel grateful to have lived — and still be living — the American Dream. I want to share it with as many as I can. I want you to know it is still possible.

I've often told the story about my son's Little League days, and one time Barbara and I went down to watch a game. The coach was telling my son's team, *"Now, I want you kids to have a good time. It's not important whether you win or lose."* I went up and told him, *"Now, wait a minute. I don't want you teaching my son that it's all right to lose. I want him to be a winner, to fight like hell and to try to win. I'd like him to learn, at this age, that America doesn't reward losers."* Barbara was pulling on my sleeve trying to get me to back off, otherwise I would still be insisting on playing to win.

Later, during my son's high school senior speech at University School, he mentioned that he remembered the story. *"My father said I don't want to learn to be a loser."* He told that story about the baseball experience because he recalled it so well, and it helped inspire him to have a winning attitude. That's an example of an early experience guiding you later in life.

If you are going to play at all, if you are in the game, be there to win. So I say, stick with it, work through it — and you will win. You don't have to be cut from some special cloth to be a successful entrepreneur.

The essence of an entrepreneur

I originally had no connection, no special interest, not anything with disabled people when Invacare came on the scene. But businesses aren't that different from each other, really. They're about different products, different settings, but it's all about delivering a superior product and fulfilling customers' needs. If you believe in your vision, you can accomplish it.

I know I am self-sustaining. I know I don't need to kiss any man's butt for what I have. I'm not dependent on anybody (except maybe Barbara) to build a business. I don't want that taken the wrong way. I've had my problems. But I am saying as far as business is concerned, I don't think I have to depend on somebody else. I can do it myself.

I tell young people each year at a class at the Case Western Reserve University Weatherhead School of Management to make their mistakes on somebody else's money. I tell them they are about to enter the most important school of all — the school of hard knocks! I worked for 11 years before I went on my own. Learning is very important. I didn't come out of a business family to go to Harvard Business School. My father didn't teach me anything about business. He taught me a lot about a lot of things, but business wasn't one of them.

206

The freedom of working for yourself is a wonderful feeling. You're not dependent on anyone. Some people are meant to be self-sufficient, and some people need to work for somebody else. When I worked for people in various jobs, I worked for some jerks and I worked for some good guys. But I was very unhappy working for a guy who wasn't as smart as I was. I could put up with it if he was a good guy, but if I had to work for someone who wouldn't keep up with me or that I was too aggressive for, I was frustrated. I'm too much of a freethinker, and I don't do everything according to the book of rules. I would think that I'm a little tougher to manage — that you really have to manage me, I suppose. I like the freedom of being my own boss where I don't have to kowtow or act politically correct or say that something is straight when I know it isn't. I'm much happier when I'm my own boss. And that's what I found at Invacare.

I think when you're an entrepreneur you control a lot of things. As you grow, you have to delegate duties because there's too much to do. I'd say release, rather than delegate. If you were working for me and I put you in charge of something, you'd be the one calling the shots. We would talk about things, but I am not going to get bogged down with all the details you have to do. You don't like to be told how to run your business. You are going to operate it yourself. You have some guidelines but you're off and running — and I've always had that attitude.

It's important to be positive and have resilience. Those are the two qualities I have always said are characteristics of an entrepreneur. As I told a panel at Case Western Reserve University recently, by being positive, you are being an optimist. I related a story about a father who had two younger children. One child was already a pessimist and the other already an optimist.

As Christmas came, the father wanted to tone down the optimistic son and kind of lift up the other one. So he gave the pessimistic son the greatest, fanciest computer he could find. He thought he'd really like it. And for the other son, he took some horse manure and put it in a red box with a red ribbon around it and gave it to him. The pessimistic son opened the computer. It didn't have the right software, it didn't have the right options — he found a lot of things wrong with his gift. He didn't like it.

Meanwhile, the other son opened his present and ran out to the pasture for about a half-hour. He came in and threw his arms around his daddy's neck and said, *"Daddy, I don't know how to thank you for this Christmas present."* The father said, *"Son, how could you be so excited about the present I gave you?"* The boy said, *"Daddy, I know there's gotta be a horse around here somewhere!"*

That to me is what an entrepreneur is all about; they are optimists and are resilient as hell. Knock 'em down; they get up. Knock 'em down again, and they get up again.

To me, an entrepreneur is a creator, a builder — not an administrator of business — and most certainly, he or she is an optimist. If I gave some executives a business to oversee, they could probably take it to the next level. It's a matter of not messing around a lot and keeping the good people you have. They are good administrators.

The entrepreneur can take something that someone else doesn't see value in and create something. Entrepreneurs almost always have their total net worth or a good part of it at risk. When they go home at night, it's not thinking about salaries and wages — it's about losing everything or winning quite a bit.

Obviously, you don't want to go back to the idea of wages or salary. I think an entrepreneur frequently can visualize a business opportunity when everybody else has given up. They tend to think outside the box and don't generally accept the conventional view. An entrepreneur, like an optimist, looks at horse crap and wonders about the possibilities.

Someone once asked me if I had a fantasy — what else I would like to do some day. If I would not have to overturn what I had, I would love to go to some far-off place with enough money in my pocket to not starve to death, with no connections and take a job as a hamburger flipper. The owner would feel pretty soon that I'm more than a hamburger flipper. He might want me as a partner. But I think a lot of people think they just have to work for someone or a company instead of being an entity unto themselves. I believe that I could again be a success from scratch. I could work my way into ownership and eventually into a situation where I could do something and have a positive outcome.

I am fortunate to be an American; there is no such thing as failing. I know men and women who tried and didn't succeed the first time around, but there is no such thing as failing.

Mal Mixon's 18 Life Lessons

1. Get an education

I thought the world was flat until I attended Harvard. Seriously, it is important to get an education if you intend to get ahead in life. The two most important things to learn in college are how to think and how to write.

I remember very little about the specific courses I took then, but the people I met, the intellectual interplay and the experience prepared me for greater things in life. Had I not gone to college, I'm sure I would have ended up just another small-town boy.

2. Serve your country

There are many ways to serve your country. In my case, I chose the U.S. Marine Corps. I thought this represented a different kind of proposition than the intellectual challenge I faced at Harvard. I thought it would make me a stronger person. It did, and as I often say, I learned more about management in the Marine Corps than I learned at Harvard Business School.

Opportunities such as the Peace Corps or serving in a political position are other ways for you to give service to your country. We are blessed to live in a free society, and each of us has an obligation to perpetuate it.

3. Know yourself

One of the greatest challenges in life is to determine what are your strengths and weaknesses. Unless you get in and mix it up in the real world to try a number of things, you will never know in which areas you excel. I'm experienced enough to know my strengths and weaknesses. I have always tried to complement my team with people who excel at things in which I do not. Find out about yourself.

4. Your word is your bond

You will go through life and build a reputation — and I think you want to have a reputation that you are as solid as a rock. You want to be known as the person who can always be counted on, who never waivers and stands tall. I learned from my father a lesson that has stayed with me for 72 years: stand up for your word. Your word will shape your reputation.

5. Make your mistakes on someone else's money

When you are a young person, you will likely make a few mistakes due to your enthusiasm and drive. As for the only perfect people in the world, the first was Jesus Christ and the other is my wife, Barbara. Otherwise, the rest of us make mistakes and have some flaws. The important thing is to not make the same mistakes twice.

I worked for 11 years for other companies before I struck out on my own. I served them well. But as I look back and remember some of the mistakes I made, I recall also learning what I would do if I ever were in charge of a company. Most young people think they know it all. Maturity is realizing that you don't.

6. Strive for excellence — be the best

From the very beginning, I always tried to be the best in anything I pursued. In some cases, I didn't achieve my goal, but I tried hard to reach it. That goes for sports, the military or business. Today, Invacare Corp. is the world leader in our field. We are 3½ times larger than our nearest competitor. We achieved this through relentless pursuit of excellence.

Invacare now is in 80 countries around the world. When we began, we were an obscure wheelchair company that the parent company was eager to dump. I frequently talked to our people about becoming the best. I don't think they believed me at first, but eventually they did and signed on to achieve it. No matter where life takes me, I try to be the best that I can be.

7. Test yourself — you may never know how good you are!

Unless you get actively involved in the real world, you'll never know how good or bad you are. You'll never know about yourself. As I related in the first chapter, one of the most difficult challenges for a country boy is to realize that he can compete with prep-school graduates from the big city.

I drove myself through many trials. I tested myself at Harvard, I tested myself in the Marine Corps on the battlefield in Vietnam, and I tested myself in business. I learned that I could achieve success. If you fail to find out about yourself, you are shortchanging yourself.

8. Harness the power of teamwork

Teamwork is the most important achievement you must develop. I learned the power of teamwork in the Marine Corps. No one is more important than another in a team.

It takes some time to learn how to build a team and how to motivate a team. People are individuals, you see. You must deal with and work with them as individuals to form a team. Each person has different ambitions, personal problems, illnesses and abilities. I feel comfortable talking with the janitor as well as the CEO of my company. Every person is important to my team. If you can deal effectively with all of these problems and challenges, your team will come to admire and respect you and want to achieve the same objectives.

9. Learn how to become a leader

Some people think that leadership is innate and cannot be learned. Others feel leadership is a collection of life's experiences. I believe in the latter. The combination of my experiences has taught me how to deal with people. You cannot lead from the rear.

10. Be tolerant of everyone you meet

The world is full of people from many different walks of life. You must learn that every idea for your company a person may suggest deserves consideration. Listen to everyone. Sometimes some of the greatest ideas come from people you least expect. But if you treat them all with respect, you will encourage ideas from everyone on how to make the company better.

Invacare is a union-free company. All associates have direct access to me. One day a female employee came into my office to complain about the appearance of the ladies restroom. I told her I have never been in the ladies restroom. So I had a woman on my staff inspect it, and in fact, the complainant was right. We promptly fixed it up, and I never heard of it being a problem again.

It all shows that if people have access to you, you aren't just sitting in an ivory tower out of touch, then more can get done. Everyone has a point of view and everyone has suggestions on how to improve the company. That's what we are really there for.

11. Have fun

We spend most of our time on the job doing one thing—working. So if you don't have fun along the way, life can be very boring. We work hard, but we enjoy each other. It's fun to build a business. It's fun to win.

I very much enjoy quail hunting, sports and playing the piano. I also like to shoot craps. All of these are entertaining for me, and I have had a good time throughout my life and career. You can't take everything too seriously. Have fun in doing whatever you do.

12. Eventually own something

I think many people do not really understand capitalism. When I was a young boy in Spiro, Okla., my teachers never once made me feel I could be an entity of my own and actually build a company. It was always, *"Who are you going to work for?"*

Even after attending Harvard Business School, I did not fully understand the concept of capitalism. It is the freedom to create something new and reach one's self-realization. There are very few people who can accumulate wealth based on salaries: athletes, movie stars, network newscasters and game show hosts, to name a few.

Once I learned my first lesson of capitalism at Invacare, I repeated it many times over, and at age 72, I still thirst for my next capitalistic venture. I've explained many of these ventures in previous chapters, and I hope to keep adding other capitalistic chapters to my life.

13. Back a good jockey

When investing in a business proposition, the most important consideration is who will run the company. It is more important than whether the idea is a good one or not. One of my friends from Cleveland, Larry Robinson, was fond of the saying that occasionally one has to make lemonade out of a lemon. A good person can frequently straighten out the darndest problems. If you are fortunate enough to have a good situation and a great jockey, you are almost 100 percent insured of success.

14. Give something back

I feel an obligation to give something back to Cleveland, Harvard and the Marine Corps because they helped develop me. For example, I give a Harvard scholarship every year to someone from Oklahoma or Northeast Ohio. I do that because I hope to help other young people from Oklahoma or Ohio much like myself who didn't have the funds to get a Harvard education. In addition, I made nearly all my money in the Cleveland area so I feel I should give my support back to the region.

I enjoy music so I supported the Mixon Hall performance site, and I'm interested in piano so I'm giving the top prize for The Cleveland International Piano Competition. I do that out of my love for music, and I want Cleveland to be the center during that event.

Anyway, Barbara and I decided that we like to give money away while we are still alive. We don't want to put it in a trust so somebody else will give it away later. We receive the pleasure of seeing the good it does. It makes us proud that we were able to support those things that are important to us.

15. Demand results

Always evaluate your people on results — not on how smart or educated they are, how they dress or whether you like them. I once had a manager who gave poor presentations and was a terrible public speaker. But I could always count on him to deliver results. On the other hand, I have had some smart, articulate MBAs who gave eloquent presentations on how and why they fell on their behinds.

16. Be consistent

One thing that can destroy an organization is an inconsistent leader. People are always asking themselves what the CEO will do in a particular situation. You do not want them to guess. You want associates and customers to trust and respect you and not become confused with double standards.

17. Attack adversity

It is easy to manage a company when things are going well. When things become challenging, some managers panic or ignore the problem altogether, hoping it will somehow go away. Instead, one should calmly lead, attack and fight for solutions. The same principle applies to one's personal challenges. Attack — don't retreat.

18. Never give up — try, try again

I have known many successful executives who did not succeed the first time around. Some of you may call that failure. I call it a temporary setback. You must pick yourself up off the floor, get back in the action and never, never give up.

The important thing is that many people don't succeed the first time they try something. You learn from the experience and then get back in the game. The same advice goes for health or other personal challenges. I had cancer. I went through the normal emotional stages of having the disease, but I got my life together physically and psychologically and was able to get back in the game.

Life does not go in a straight line. You are going to have challenges. Find your way through your problems. The important thing is to get through those challenges — and by never giving up, you will triumph.

Epilogue: Mal Mixon, the Alchemist - By Dennis Seeds

What others have to say about Mal Mixon, who is probably most well-known for his 1979 leveraged buyout of wheelchair manufacturer Invacare and other investments, is the stuff of legends. Nobody can better define the essence of Mal Mixon as a person than those who made the following comments. They are some who know him best — who have seen him, so to speak, turn something of lesser value into gold.

-:-

Mal Mixon wants other people to have what he has had — success. He really wants people to win. — Bill Weber, CEO of Air Enterprises LLC

-:-

He's involved not only with his company but with related business activities, in health care and with people in the community. He's deeply involved with everything that he does. His involvement has contributed to his business acumen and, of course, his good judgment. Perhaps, secondarily, but equally as descriptive as involved, is that he has great loyalty to the people who he works with. — Dr. Floyd Loop, former CEO of Cleveland Clinic

-:-

When he sees an opportunity he just goes at it with a sense of determination, a sense of creativity, an ability to collaborate and just sheer fortitude. He sees his way through all obstacles to make it successful. — Baiju Shah. Shah is the founder, former president and CEO of the nonprofit BioEnterprises and is now the CEO of BioMotiv.

-:-

He is willing to take on most any problem or project, whether personal, political or business. He has a lot of vision and is always thinking one step ahead — he's never satisfied with the status quo. — Barbara Mixon, Mal's wife

-:-

Mal is able to instantaneously distinguish between the talk and the walk and has a clear sense of the real potential for achievement. His success, as with any great leader, is the ability to recognize honesty combined with talent and reward it with responsibility. — Joel Smirnoff, president of the Cleveland Institute of Music

-:-

He has the ability to lead even in the face of adversity. — J.B. Richey, engineer and Mal's longtime friend and partner

-:-

Mal's personality is like … he makes big bets, goes to bed and sleeps like a baby. I don't know if it's nature or nurture, but Mal was born with the DNA to embrace risk. — Mark Mansour, senior managing partner of MCM Capital Partners

-:-

He has an uncompromising loyalty to others. When the grenades start landing, you don't have to look around to see if Mal is still there. — Richard Osborne, professor at Case Western Reserve University Weatherhead School of Management

-:-

When you first meet Mal Mixon it's probably going to be a very memorable experience. You just might be taken with his unfiltered candor as he speaks his mind, his hearty laugh and his command of the room.

The eight comments above represent the thoughts and feelings not only of longtime acquaintances of 35-plus years but also of others with only a third of that many years of friendship. It's an easy task to conclude that Mixon has the ability to impress anyone of any age.

Bill Weber, at the time a commercial real estate entrepreneur, answered his phone one Sunday evening. It was Mal.

"He had a real estate question and just talking to him over the phone, I kind of sensed he wanted to talk more about it. I said, 'Would it help if I came over?' and he said, 'That'd be great.' So I left the house and my wife said, 'What's going on here? It's Sunday night!' But he always had that kind of ability to make people help him, and it's funny. It's a strange quality. You don't know quite why, but you end up wanting to do something for him, so I went down there that night. We spent time on the project, and he was comfortable, and I ended up doing Invacare's real estate work as a result."

"There is kind of magnetism about him. He would, in some mysterious way, get people to help him and do more for him and his causes, which is kind of an obvious leadership quality. I never quite figured out how he did it. Ha ha! But I think if you ask people, they would confirm that."

Mark Mansour got to know Mal through an introduction from his father Ernie Mansour, who has been one of Mal's lawyers. But it took the offer of a business deal that really got Mal and Mark on the same wavelength.

"A friend of mine called and asked if I would help raise capital to try to buy the business that he was running," Mansour says. *"We had a few days to put together a write-up on the company and see if we could interest*

anybody without really any knowledge of the people, the business or any due diligence to support management team efforts in buying this business.

"Within 48 hours we had put together an offering memorandum, which I sent out to people whom I thought may have the risk appetite along with the financial resources to support a bid." Mal Mixon was one of those people. Mal was building a local reputation as a very successful private investor as well as successfully running Invacare. So Mal called me back almost immediately saying, 'Be at my house Saturday morning.'

"I showed up at his house with the operator of this business, and we pitched the story to Mal." He said, *"I like it. I like the company, and I like the opportunity. I'll commit.'* He and his buddies committed to $3 million of capital after a half-hour meeting! I was a 32-year-old guy who Mal didn't really know. He knew my father — he didn't know me. And he certainly didn't know the management team, and he didn't know the company, but that sort of typifies Mal. He has a big risk appetite, and he relies on his gut feeling. More often than not, he's right."*

"Talking about taking risks, he didn't know if I was talented or untalented or anything like that, and after that Saturday meeting, he called me back and said, 'Look, I'd like to get together with you,'" Mansour says. *"Then he pitched the idea of forming MCM Capital. 'I'd like you to run it,' he said. I had not done anything in my career to demonstrate that I can effectively run a fund, but, again, Mal, A.) he went ahead based on a gut feel, and B.) he had the right risk appetite and profile. So he took a huge risk on me, and for that I'll forever be grateful."*

-:-

If there is one thing that sets Mal apart from others is that so few of his friends and business partners seem to identify the same distinguishing attribute — but everyone can name some impressive quality.

"I always looked at intellect, different kinds of intellect, different kinds of intelligence," Bill Weber says about Mal Mixon. *"There's common sense, there's memory, there's how people rationalize, there are people skills, there's a whole bunch of different kinds of intellect."*

"I have never seen in my life someone who had such a full complement of all of those different intellects. Underneath it, he's an incredible strategic thinker. Yet his people skills really set him apart, and I think his memory, he has an outstanding memory. He can recall all kinds of events and tell stories."

"He has a unique leadership ability, which I think is a form of intellect. What other kind of intellect is there? Common sense — I have never seen that much in another person in my life. He can go into a redneck bar, and he'll make friends in 10 minutes and then he could be in the president's, a congressman's or senator's office and he's the same guy making more friends. So, his people skills, memory, intellect, rationalization, leadership — you name it, Mal's got it."

Dr. Floyd Loop feels Mal has an unbeatable combination.

"I think first, he has relentless drive. His enthusiasm for whatever project is at hand is almost infectious," Loop says. *"As everyone will tell you, he has an unparalleled entrepreneurial spirit. So I would, to make that as succinct as I could, think that combination, that confluence of characteristics, sets him apart from most people."*

Joel Smirnoff of the Cleveland Institute of Music notes how Mal's people-sense is a key factor in his personality.

"Mal has a deep sense of people and of their various personalities and qualities," he says. *"Mal has, to this day, a very quick sense of who is in the room, reading people extremely well and immediately. He is able to instantaneously distinguish between the talk and the walk and has a clear sense of the real potential for achievement. His success, as with any great*

leader, is the ability to recognize honesty combined with talent and reward it with responsibility. Mal also knows the preciousness of time and how frugally it needs to be spent."

"What sets Mal apart is not in the visual manner but in the figurative manner. There's just not another way to put it," says Baiju Shah.

"He is larger than life. I mean, here's a guy who's done many things. In everything he does, he does not believe he'll fail. When he sees an opportunity, he just goes at it with determination, a sense of creativity and an ability to collaborate, and with sheer fortitude. He sees his way through all the obstacles to make it successful. And, obviously, he's done that, not just with Invacare, but what I admire is he's done it with so many other ventures. Then he's mentored people like me, and many other entrepreneurs throughout, not just Cleveland, on how to help launch their ventures."

"Another thing that I think really sets Mal apart from many people is his willingness to help others be successful and his personal time," Shah says. *"It's a huge investment but it's not financial; it's really his time, his energy and his contacts. He wants to make sure it's successful. He wants to make sure the person he's helping will be successful. He's full of energy. He doesn't stop."*

"The other thing that I think, there are two other dimensions that make Mal very different," Shah says. *"He truly is committed to the community. You see this in so many different ways, whether it's his leadership of institutions like the Cleveland Clinic or the Cleveland Institute of Music. He didn't get paid to do any of these things."*

"In fact, in many cases, it's a negative payment. He's making contributions on top of leading these institutions. He doesn't just get involved, he wants to really be involved, and because he cares so passionately about his community, the thrust of activities is much larger than people would recognize."

"But he's also been instrumental in a number of minority funds to give disadvantaged groups opportunities," Shah says. *"He was the driving*

force behind Minorities with Vision, the $25 million special venture fund for minority- and women-run businesses. He's a driving force in politics. He's obviously advocating for good health care policy, but at the community level, local as well as state, that's just about creating a good environment for growing our space."

"He is a leader in really driving for good policy. He'll tell you that he doesn't like to be labeled one or the other. He just wants good solid policy being done that creates an environment in which businesses and individuals really have the opportunity to succeed."

Richard Osborne, Weatherhead School of Management professor, says one thing simply sets Mal apart: his courage.

Osborne plans to use him in his CEO course in spring 2013. Mal will be the subject for his class to do an in-depth study of his professional career and success. Some of those who Mal personally has invited to participate in the class include businessman Dan Moore, Cleveland Clinic CEO Delos *"Toby"* Cosgrove and Invacare CEO Gerry Blouch.

Each student will be expected to write a 2,500-3,000-word article that captures what he or she has learned about Mixon. This assignment will account for a big portion of their grade so they will be highly motivated to do a good job.

"Mal has a wonderful, inspiring story," Osborne says. *"I'm anxious for my students to benefit from the lessons of his life and the values by which he lives."*

J.B. Richey, his longtime friend and business partner, says certain outstanding qualities separate Mal from others: *"His loyalty, high integrity, smart business savvy, strategic thinking, he's responsive, dynamic, do-it-now, ethical, optimistic and tireless, like the Energizer Bunny."*

-:-

Often a person is judged by the contributions he or she makes to society. In Mal's case the contributions are not only many tangibles but intangibles as well.

"It's how he's helped so many people," says Bill Weber. *"He's helped them with their causes or their companies, and it's the number of people that he's assisted. He helped Fred Loop. He helped Toby Cosgrove. He's helped all these little companies. He's also helped venture firms that he's been involved with. I mean the breadth of people that he's helped is really outstanding, and I think it has had a significant impact on the community. He's given back money, but I think more it's the guidance, advice and support that he's given all these people is the most significant contribution."*

Mixon's wide range of expertise in many areas impresses many. His lifelong interest in learning is obvious but not ostentatious.

"As a Renaissance man, he's also very interested in the community, the people and particularly the arts," Loop says. *"But because he has this multidimensional brain and all the talent that goes along with it, he's been able to contribute a lot to the community just by helping people through his philanthropy. His contribution to the arts and his interest in contributions to health care are very impressive.*

"There are very few trustees of medical institutions that actually have a deep interest in the organization, and Mal certainly has had that. He is highly engaged with everything he is interested in, not only to the business but apart from the business: the arts, community, people. So, whenever Mal leaves a project, the people that are there to take up the responsibilities that he had held for so long find it very, very difficult to replace him."

Baiju Shah noticed how Mal Mixon has been deeply involved in the community but in a quiet manner.

"I think Mal's biggest contribution has been the impact he had on people in Cleveland, whether these are his leaders at Invacare, independent

businesses that he's been involved and invested in, nonprofit leaders like myself, the Cleveland Clinic or the Cleveland Institute of Music," he says. *"His eagerness to mentor others and support their ability to be successful — I don't think people recognize that a lot of other things that they might see in the community in many ways trace themselves back to Mal's leadership."*

"That's the sort of an impact Mal has had on people because he's a very humble guy. He has no desire to be out in front taking credit. It's not all of these different things he does; it's just that he does it his own way, involved, forceful but quiet. I think that that is one of his greatest legacies — his network who can all trace themselves back in some way to Mal."

-:-

Mal even surprises his inner circle — who should know him well — with some of his hidden talents and skills.

"First of all, his background, if you know, is that of a salesman, and he is as close to being the consummate salesman that I've ever met," Loop says. *"It surprised me how effective he is as a salesman, which helped him in all of his many projects. He's emotionally involved with everything he takes up. He's fascinated by the projects. I think he has a great interest in learning more about each project that he's part of."*

"One thing surprising is that he's got a great sense of humor," Shah says. *"He's got humility about himself. He's just a very down-to-earth individual. You may get the impressions that a CEO of a Fortune 1000 company must have all sorts of different behaviors, but you get to know Mal, and he is really fun-loving; he does not take himself seriously as an individual and doesn't like anybody who does, and he doesn't like anybody who puts on airs."*

"Mal is extremely sensitive and I have seen him go out of his way to help someone who is faltering to find his or her way," Smirnoff says. *"I don't know if it is surprising, but it is certainly not the first trait that*

comes to mind in a Marine or former Marine. Mal is a deeply caring person who enjoys reflecting on the human drama and its tragic and comic manifestations. His deep love for music is an expression of that."

"Mal Mixon has contributed in a lasting way through both his life's work and his generosity toward raising the quality of life for people who may never get to meet him, but who nevertheless get to enjoy the beneficent effect of his conscious and purposeful actions on their behalf."

-:-

What one word describes Mal Mixon?

Entrepreneurial, inspiring, observant, a real tour de force.
— *Baiju Shah*

Gifted would have to be one of many words. I mean he really is gifted.
— *Bill Weber*

Loyal, how incredibly loyal he is to every one of his close associates.
— *Mark Mansour*

Fearless. He is not afraid of anything, including success and failure.
— *Richard Osborne*

Real. Mal will always be straight with you, which will make the weak uncomfortable and the strong more engaged.
— *Joel Smirnoff*

My best friend.
— *J.B. Richey*

He is indomitable. It never occurs to him that something can't be done; he just tries to figure out how it can be done.
— *Barbara Mixon*